Very Intentional Parenting

Awakening the Empowered Parent Within

Very Intentional Parenting

Awakening the
Empowered
Parent Within

DESTINI ANN DAVIS

Publisher Mike Sanders
Senior Editor Brook Farling
Art & Design Director William Thomas
Assistant Director of Art & Design Rebecca Batchelor
Compositor Ayanna Lacey
Proofreader Amy J. Schneider
Indexer Johnna VanHoose Dinse

First American Edition, 2022
Published in the United States by DK Publishing
6081 E. 82nd Street, Indianapolis, Indiana 46250
Copyright © 2022 Destini Ann Davis
22 23 24 25   10 9 8 7 6 5 4 3 2 1
001-328441-AUG2022
All rights reserved.

Note: This publication contains the opinions and ideas of its author. It is intended
to provide helpful and informative material on the subject matter covered. It is
sold with the understanding that the author and publisher are not engaged in
rendering professional services in the book. If the reader requires personal
assistance or advice, a competent professional should be consulted. The author
and publisher specifically disclaim any responsibility for any liability, loss, or risk,
personal or otherwise, which is incurred as a consequence, directly or indirectly,
of the use and application of any of the contents of this book.

Trademarks: All terms mentioned in this book that are known to be or are
suspected of being trademarks or service marks have been appropriately
capitalized. Alpha Books, DK, and Penguin Random House LLC cannot attest to
the accuracy of this information. Use of a term in this book should not be regarded
as affecting the validity of any trademark or service mark.

Library of Congress Catalog Number: 2022931014
ISBN: 978-0-7440-5706-5

DK books are available at special discounts when purchased in bulk for sales
promotions, premiums, fund-raising, or educational use. For details, contact:
SpecialSales@dk.com
Printed and bound in the United States of America

Author photos © Demel Bolden

For the curious
www.dk.com

Contents

Foreword

I met Destini Ann in September of 2021 after following her on Instagram for weeks and feeling truly enamored with her ability to express complex topics in understandable language. I remember the day that my business partner and I were watching her reels and saying to each other, "Wow, she's amazing. We're obsessed with her. Let's figure out how to work together in some way!" Then, truly only hours later, I opened Instagram to see this first direct message from Destini: "Someone referred me to your page. I'm obsessed. I'd love to collaborate on something if you're ever interested." And here we are, one year from that first connection. What began between Destini and me as a mutual admiration society is now something deeper and more special: Destini is someone I consider a true colleague, thought partner, and friend.

And so, you may be wondering, who am I? First, let me introduce myself: my name is Dr. Becky Kennedy, and I'm a clinical psychologist specializing in parenting, anxiety, and resilience. I am also a mother of three, an early riser, and a forever learner. And that last phrase, "forever learner," is probably at the core of my identity. There's nothing that gives me as much purpose or joy as thinking, considering new ideas, and problem solving about tricky dynamics in family systems. Over the past two years, I've developed *Good Inside*—a new approach to help parents manage the struggles in their homes. *Good Inside* is based on my core belief that we are all, well, good inside, and we are all doing the best we can with the resources we have available in the moment. And yet, parenting from a *Good Inside* perspective is not an "anything goes" or "soft" method. Yes, it requires us to tap into validation and empathy, but it also requires us to embody our authority and set firm boundaries.

So how does one "do" *Good Inside* parenting? Well, it starts with a commitment to oneself. Yes, that's right: *Good Inside* parents know that they cannot give out what they have not given in; in other words, they know that parenting is a journey of self-discovery and

Foreword

that the more they work on their triggers and their coping skills, the more they *and* their kids will benefit. This isn't selfish. It is simply effective as kids develop in the context of their relationship with their parents. And so, the sturdier a parent is, the safer a child feels, and that safety allows for healthy development.

What does it mean that children develop in the context of their relationships with their parents? Glad you asked! This is an important one, and it's something that's at the heart of my approach and also Destini's. Kids don't learn how to cope with emotions from school or a book; kids learn how to cope with emotions through their experiences with their parents. In other words, a child learns to manage strong feelings, safely express anger, and tolerate frustration (all massively important life skills!) by absorbing what happens in their family homes during emotional moments. Here's what this looks like in real life: as your child is having a tantrum, they are taking in *your reaction* to their tantrum and whether it's possible to be calm amidst a swirl of big feelings. So yes, parenting "strategies" and "scripts" are useful. Still, it is even more useful to remember that more than anything else, a child's emotion regulation development comes from our *relationship with them during tough moments.*

And why does emotion regulation matter so much? Aren't emotions kind of "soft" compared to the important "hard" skills in life? If you're wondering this, you're not alone. I hear this all the time from parents! I hear things like, "I'm just not a 'feelings' person. I focus on the important stuff in life," or "My family never helped me with my feelings, and I turned out just fine." I get it. I really do! And I'm not here to convince, but rather to just present how I see it. To me, emotion regulation—the ability to manage one's feelings—is not some soft or nice-to-have skill; by contrast, I see emotion regulation as the single most important skill to develop throughout our lives. After all, emotion regulation is at the core of how we function throughout adulthood. When it comes to dealing with getting fired from a job, we lean on our emotion regulation skills; when it comes to talking to a partner about something we need from them, we need our emotion regulation skills; when it comes to telling someone, "No, I don't like that. Stop right now," we need our emotion regulation skills. Emotions are at the core of who we are, and emotion regulation is at the core of how we function. After all, our mental health comes from our ability to manage the emotional demands of life. While it is never too late to develop one's emotion regulation skills further, helping our kids develop these skills *early* is the most powerful gift we can give them.

Now let's get real: if you're like most adults, right now you may be thinking, "Hmm… okay… maybe this makes sense, but how can I give my child emotion regulation skills if no one helped give these skills to me? How can I be the type of parent for my child that I want to be if I never had this type of parenting modeled for me?" And then you may jump to this thought: "I'm too tired. I can't do this." Whether you are in "How can I be this type of parent" mode or "This feels too overwhelming" mode, you're in luck. Why? Because you now have Destini's book, which takes big concepts and breaks them down into relatable language and manageable steps. Destini is a parent coach who is also your biggest cheerleader. So keep reading.

Destini gets it. She has a way of blending sophisticated topics with authentic examples and a realistic tone. She knows firsthand how hard parenting is and how hard it is to change your parenting approach. So if she's explaining how to manage a tantrum, it's because she just managed a tantrum; if she's sharing how to manage your own feelings, it's because she is still working to manage her *own* big feelings. Destini is like that wise (and fun!) friend you always want to have lunch with. She offers knowledge without judgment and advice without superiority. She believes in you, truly, because she knows what it's like to feel down on oneself and what it takes to turn that feeling around. Destini will help you feel better about your parenting, but she'll also help you feel better about *yourself.*

Foreword

After all my years in training and practice and after working with thousands of families, here's something I know with utter confidence: parenting is hard. It's hard for you, it's hard for Destini, and it's hard for me. And it's not your fault that parenting feels hard. As I often say, it feels hard because it is hard! We are supposed to feel things as they are. And yet, at the same time, this is true too: parenting can be joyful. Not all the time, but definitely more of the time. And so we are left with this: parenting is hard *and* parenting can bring joy. One isn't more true than the other; instead, two things are true. And here's something else I know: right now, it's probably really hard to find the joy in parenting. This doesn't make you a bad parent. On the contrary, this makes you a perfect fit for the journey ahead in this book. You're in the right place. And you have the right leader here in Destini. So with all of that in mind, let's jump in.

Dr. Becky Kennedy

Introduction

They called it "Honesty Hour for Moms."

I sat down on what was, hands down, the nicest couch I'd ever seen. We'll call it cashmere, but I honestly have no clue what material I was disgracing with my ripped thrift store jeans. Silly me! I must have missed the "wear your best outfit" memo.

I've never seen whites so white or creases so creased. These women did not come to play. But there I was with an unidentifiable stain on my NSYNC T-shirt… yeah.

Now, there are moments when you feel like a glorious unicorn in a field of common horses—like you walked in and everyone instantly thought, "Damn… why didn't I bring a glitter horn?"

Well, let me tell you, this was not my majestic unicorn moment. It was more like someone invited Little Orphan Annie to the Met Gala and said, "Come as you are."

Not only was I underdressed, but I was clearly underprepared for the next 60 minutes of my life. I sat up on that fancy couch, took a deep breath, and tried to release any judgment.

No, for real. I tried really hard to have an open mind.

But somewhere between "Hello, mom friend" and "Do you have a Pinterest?" I knew damn well this was not about to be the "Honesty Hour for Moms" Facebook had advertised! (Thanks for nothing, social media.) So, for the next 60 minutes I listened to my new "mom friends" complain about parenting struggles that I'd literally pay to have.

I heard everything from "My toddler almost stressed me out this morning!" to "I haven't washed clothes in two days." I mean, call me insensitive, but come on… two days?! You're freakin' killin' it! And you almost got stressed? Ha! I don't even think I have an "almost" emotion.

Introduction

Now, by no means am I trying to make light of their struggles, because I could see in their caffeine-buzzed eyes that they had bigger struggles, too! And I thought, "If a circle of moms isn't the best place to be real about motherhood, what is?" It got me thinking: If they can't even be honest with other moms, who the heck are they being honest with? Who are they talking to about the 3 a.m. night terrors? Or not having an answer for "Can I make Puppy come back alive?" Are they just sitting with the guilt and shame and stress that comes with mothering in the age of social media? Or worse, are they perpetuating the guilt, shame, and stress of today's parenting challenges with things like this bullshit "honesty hour"?

And so on that day, I decided to share my authentic journey more openly. I started posting online about my challenges and the resources that have made me a better mother. Through this journey, I've met so many incredible parents and I've gained so much support. What I'm most proud of is how much my journey has empowered so many other parents and caregivers to be their best selves. Though I couldn't wait to leave that catastrophe of a "mommy meetup," I am grateful for the path it set me on. Now, as a parenting coach, I get to create an authentic community for parents to share their experiences in a vulnerable way. My platform has become an *actual* honesty hour! Together, we are healing intergenerational wounds, reparenting ourselves, learning new skills, and building the most amazing connections with our kids. This is intentional parenting! It's about reclaiming our identities as caregivers. We get to be curious about what's not "working" and create the narratives that support the family dynamics we truly desire. And guess what? I want to invite you into this community. I want to take this journey with you. I want to support you as you peel back the layers, excavate your power, and become the intentional parent you are meant to be.

In my online community, I spend a lot of time talking about the self-awareness that is required to be an intentional parent. Intentional parents come in many different forms: some are very organized and meticulous, creating complex schedules and enrolling their kids in the best institutions; others are spontaneous and free, allowing their children to discover life organically. Some moms discipline their kids with a serious tone and by counting to 10, while others choose "time-in" corners and positive reinforcement. But intentional parenting is not just about the specific choices we make. Rather, it's about making conscious choices from a place of power. When we focus solely on our children's behaviors, we give that power away. Parenting is leadership.

It's my hope that through this book, you will learn how to keep your parenting power.

Hear me clearly: you are doin' a good job! You are the kind of parent who reads parenting books, for goodness' sake! And now is your opportunity to take it to the next level. You get to move into empowerment. You get to show up as the relentless table shaker who takes radical responsibility for your family. You get to grab the bull by the horns and be the change in your home. This doesn't mean you ignore your children's behaviors or shame yourself when you mess up. It's quite the opposite. By taking responsibility, you are choosing to make decisions that align with your values. This positive step will help guide your children's behaviors and also help keep you out of the shame cycle that comes from parenting without intention.

Are you down? Well, you bought this book, so I sure as hell hope so!

Part 1
Radical Responsibility

As a parenting coach, I get countless questions. They are all over the place and address a wide range of topics, from toddler hitting to dealing with an uncooperative co-parent. Some parents reach out simply because they're looking for ways to make life easier. They rarely have time for themselves because they're overwhelmed with their kids, their spouses, and their mile-high to-do lists. They feel unappreciated and spend countless hours picking up after their kids, repeating themselves, and handing out punishments.

All of these questions have brought me to a very clear conclusion—parents are desperately seeking ways to change their child's behavior. For a while I only approached these kinds of questions with constructive advice. I thought, "These parents need help. They need resources." So I dug into my toolkit and began helping my community. I leaned on all of the research I've done and the training I've received on parenting and developmental psychology to offer realistic solutions for the problems they were facing. At first, this seemed like a great approach. Many of the research-based strategies I use are extremely impactful, and I started getting messages about how well and how quickly they were working. But then something interesting happened. The same parents kept returning day after day with more questions about their children's behaviors.

And that's when it hit me. All of the parenting tips and tools mean nothing if you don't start with what I now see as the most important piece of the puzzle—the parent. You have so much power! You are actually the expert in your family. And how you show up to the parenting journey has the greatest impact on whether or not you can spark real and lasting change. Sure, your life would be easier if your 8-year-old would just stop talking back. But managing the chaos is a lot easier when we focus on our own emotions, beliefs, and behaviors first. So this is where we're starting. Not with tips to keep the toddler in his bed or with advice for dealing with the kid who won't do her homework. We're starting with personal responsibility—a Radical Responsibility to enact change within ourselves. So in order to create lasting change in the dynamics of your family, we're going to first start with the behaviors of the one person you can control: *you*.

1

Setting Your Intentions

When you get in your car, you don't just say "Hey Siri, take me there!" or "Hey Siri, put me around this area." No, you type in a specific destination. So, as you begin to reclaim your power and shift the dynamics in your family, you will need to clearly define your destination. As you learn to be the guide who was sent here to help your child thrive, you will need something to be tethered to. Of course, you won't always know which way to go or what route to take. Sometimes, there will be roadblocks and detours, and all sorts of annoying delays on your journey. But having a clear destination for your parenting intentions will keep you on course.

My Parenting Intention

I don't always have the right words or the right tools for every moment. But what I do have is a deep understanding of my beliefs and what my desires are for my family. When my three-year-old started hitting (something I never experienced with my oldest), I remembered my intention and responded with compassion for her. When my oldest, in her anger, told me she hated me,

I remembered my intention and responded with compassion for her. When I was going through my divorce and hit rock bottom, I remembered my intention and responded with compassion for myself.

I'll be honest, there are moments when I feel completely discouraged and disconnected from my role as a mother. Even as I'm writing this book, I'm going through one of the toughest seasons in my life. My intention for my family is what I'm anchored in—it's why I practice breathing when I want to yell. It's why I see our family challenges as opportunities for us to grow. It's why I continue to be gentle with myself when I'm late for the play date or when I lose my patience. Sometimes it feels like I'm walking slowly with my eyes closed and my hands tied behind my back. But my intention for my family is quite literally what keeps me walking in the right direction. This is the start of intentional parenting—knowing who you are, where you want to go, and what you value. These are the things that make up your intention for yourself and your family.

Your Parenting Intention

The following sections are some gentle reminders for defining your journey, along with a few questions to help you uncover your personal parenting intention. So it's time to grab your journal or notebook and begin doing the work. Take time to think and write down your answers. (This book is interactive for one main reason: if you don't do the work, I'll end up doing it for you. I don't want you to just take my insights and make them your own, I want you to take the knowledge I give you and use it to bring out all of the powerful tools you already have inside yourself.) This section, like the rest of the book, is an excavation process. We are digging out all of your greatness so that you can serve your family authentically.

Reminder: You Deserve to Be Celebrated

None of us get it right all the time. I promise you that! I want to yell almost every single day. And I don't always have the compassion my kids deserve; I'm not always fun, playful, or excited about being a parent. But I'm getting better. And better is *fantastic*. Better is more than enough. Perfection is bullshit! It's crippling because it forces you to believe that some end goal has more value than where you currently are, and that's just not true. You've already broken some generational cycles. You've already done some healing. You're already giving your kids so many great skills and tools. And that all deserves to be celebrated. *You* deserve to be celebrated. You are the kind of parent who reads parenting books. You are amazing already!

So consider the productive ways you are already parenting with power and intention. These will be the building blocks for your success as a parent. A lot of times we get so caught up in what's not working, but the best place to start creating your parenting intention is with an honest evaluation of what *is* working! This will empower you to keep striving toward confidence and ease in your parenting.

Ask yourself:

- What do you love about yourself as a parent?
- What do you love about your family?
- What is something you love about parenting?
- What simple pleasures do you and your family enjoy?
- What was a parenting win this week?
- What are your strengths as a parent?
- What strengths do you notice about your family?

Reminder: Challenges Are How You Grow

I've reminded you to celebrate yourself and that is a really important step when you're measuring personal progress. However, that's not the whole picture. In order to really see your progress, you also have to be willing to look at your challenges. By seeing where you've been and where you're currently at, you'll be able to better measure your progress over time.

Some days are going to be a complete shit show. You're not always going to know what to do or what to say. And you will face challenges that will test you. In those moments where you feel completely defeated, I want you to remember this: you can learn anything and you can develop new skills to support yourself and your family. Taking a growth mindset is going to be one of your greatest assets on this journey, so start looking at challenges as growth opportunities. When your child is screaming in the middle of the store, that is an opportunity to increase your tolerance for discomfort. When your child's heart is broken because they got picked last at school, that is an opportunity to increase your compassion. Every step of the way, you'll have opportunities to increase your knowledge, kindness, respect, emotional intelligence, patience, and so many other things. Our children, if we let them, give us the opportunity to expand into more conscious, intentional humans. It is in the messiness that you'll have the opportunity to become the best version of yourself.

Ask yourself:

- What are your current challenges as a parent?
- How do you typically respond to challenges?
- What are your fears in parenting?
- Who or what supports you through your challenges?
- Do you ever feel confused, lost, stuck?
- What aspects of parenting do you feel you need more support or more information on?

Reminder: Your Values Will Guide You

There are very few things in parenting that are actually right or wrong, or good or bad. Rather, we simply all have our own opinions that are based on our values. This means that no one gets to tell you what is or isn't right for your family. *You* get to decide. Some parents choose to sleep train their kids, while others co-sleep with their kids. Some parents find a lot of value in formal academics while others prioritize learning through experience. I'm not here to tell you what should matter to you, I simply want to encourage you to make parenting decisions that are rooted in your personal values—not in fear, other people's opinions, or your own ego. Intentional parenting means parenting from the essence of who you truly are. When you do that, it's so much easier to parent with confidence and to trust the process. It's when we parent in ways that are out of alignment with our personal truth that we feel insecure.

In the moments that you don't know what to do, return to your values. When you make a decision and something just doesn't feel right, ask yourself "Does this go against my values?" When you get parenting advice, crosscheck it against your values.

Now you may have never taken the time to actually think about what your values are. Or maybe you already make values-based decisions, but for some reason you still don't feel confident in your path. Or maybe you already make values-based decisions and you parent with consciousness and intention. Either way, let's take some time to define, clarify, or revisit your values!

Ask yourself:

- What kinds of things make you smile?
- What kinds of things make you feel frustrated?
- If you could do one thing all day, what would it be?
- When do you feel safe?
- Do you ever feel embarrassed? When?

- What makes you feel special?

- What are you good at?

- What do you wish you were better at?

- Who are your heroes? Who do you admire? What do they do that you find admirable?

- How do you think other people should be treated?

- How do you think you should be treated?

- What are five things that are really important to you?

- What do you like to do with the people closest to you?

- What is something that you absolutely cannot stand?

- What do you like to do by yourself?

- What makes you feel nervous?

- When was a time when you felt super excited?

- When do you feel calm or peaceful?

- If you could change one thing about the world, what would it be?

Finish the exercise by completing this statement: "I love _____."
(Write the first thing that comes to mind)

As you review the answers to the preceding questions, consider the following list of possible values and choose 15 that resonate most with you. (You can also add your own if you don't see them on the list.)

Acceptance	Adaptability
Achievement	Adventure
Accountability	Authenticity
Acquisition of money	Beauty

1 Setting Your Intentions

Calm

Challenge

Change

Charity

Cleanliness

Compassion

Competition

Connection

Consistency

Cooperation

Courage

Courteousness

Creativity

Curiosity

Discipline

Determination

Equality

Excellence

Excitement

Fairness

Faith

Family

Financial stability

Freedom

Friendship

Fun

Generational wealth

Generosity

Global awareness

Goodwill

Gratitude

Growth

Happiness

Hard work

Health

Honesty

Honor

Humility

Humor

Independence

Individuality

Inner peace

Innovation

Integrity

Intelligence

Intimacy

Justice

Kindness

Knowledge

Leadership

Legacy

Love

Loyalty

Meaning

Nonviolence

Open-mindedness

Openness

Order

Patriotism

Peace

Perfection

Perseverance

Personal development

Personal growth

Philanthropy

Pleasure

Power

Preservation

Privacy

Progress

Prosperity

Punctuality

Quality

Quiet

Regularity

Reliability

Resourcefulness

Respect

Romance

Safety

Security

Self-awareness

Self-care

Self-improvement

Self-love

Sensitivity

Service

Simplicity

Skillfulness

Social status

Solitude

Spirituality

Stability

Status

Strength

Success

Teamwork

Tolerance

Tradition

Trust

Truth

Unity

Well-being

1 Setting Your Intentions

Once you've created your list of 15 core values, answer the following questions about each value.

1. How long have you had this value?

2. Where did this value come from?

3. How often do you model this value? (Often? Sometimes? Rarely?)

4. Say to yourself "_____ is really important to me." How do you feel when you hear this? Does this statement feel true? Untrue? Natural? Forced? Uncomfortable?

5. Can you describe an instance when you've chosen this value over something else?

In completing this exercise, you will gain a better grasp on what really matters to you. Once you've narrowed down your list, I invite you to further narrow your list down to the three that resonate with you the most. (You'll need these later in the process when you clarify your intention, but for now, just jot them down.)

Before you move on, it's important to remember a few things about your values. First, your values may change as you learn and grow, so this list may shift. You should feel free to return to this practice whenever you feel especially out of alignment or insecure in your parenting.

Second, it's important to be honest with yourself when defining your values. The more comfortable you are with your true values, the easier it will be for you to respect and honor your child's values. Because, guess what? They're not you. Though you're doing the work of intentional modeling, they will inevitably write their own story. So in order to accept the truth of who they are, you first have to accept the truth of who you are. So be honest with yourself about what you value and recognize when something is a true value versus a desired value. For example, I really wish I valued order and organization. I think my life would be so much easier if I just had a desire to clean my house every day! But I don't—like, not at all. There are so many things I value more than order and organization, and it's evident in the things that I choose over them. If I parent from my desired values, I will make hypocritical decisions and struggle to gain my children's respect. (Imagine me constantly yelling about their clothes on the floor. Ha!) Now it doesn't mean I don't encourage them to clean their rooms, I definitely do, but it's certainly not a focus in my house. And if I want it to be, then I have to first develop that value within myself before I expect to instill it in my children.

Lastly, no value is better than another. Your values are not wrong. They're just... your values. A mom whose top value is kindness is not a better parent than a mom whose top value is wealth. (Read that last sentence again.) We all have different experiences that shape who we are. It's okay if you have different values than your parents, your neighbors, or even your friends. In fact, it's not just okay, it's a relief. Thank goodness we don't all have to think alike!

Reminder: You Get to Create Your Own Parenting Intention

Now that you have a good sense of who you are as a parent, it's time to create who you'd like to be! (You'll want to return to this exercise as you read through this book.) Creating personal goals will allow you to apply the information in this book in a way that feels authentic to your journey. I don't want to create carbon copies of the parent I am. Rather, I want to empower you to become the parent that *you* desire to be. So it's important to clarify exactly who that parent is!

Ask yourself:

• How do you *want* to feel as a parent?

1 Setting Your Intentions

- What are the general emotional states you would like to experience in your parenting? (Happiness? Excitement? Joy? Peace?)

- How would you like to be described as a parent?

- What do you want your children to thank you for?

- What are three to five parenting goals for this year?

- What is one parenting goal for this month?

Now let's piece it all together to create a tangible representation of everything we've just uncovered. This will be your *parenting intention*. It's important that you do this before you read any further in the book. If you aren't able to write these responses out right now, put the book down and come back to complete this exercise when you have time. By doing so, you'll be able to consistently return to your parenting intention to support your goals.

Answer these questions to define your parenting intention:

- I am _____.
  (List things you love about yourself.)

- I am _____.
  (List your strengths as a parent.)

- Sometimes, I struggle with _____.
  (List your challenges.)

- When I am challenged, I typically respond by _____.

- When I need support, I can _____.

- My top three values are _____, _____, and _____.

- I actively strive to model and encourage these values in my home.

- The kind of parent I strive to be is
  _____. I will work daily to be
  this kind of parent.

- Because I want to feel _____,
  this year I will work on the following goals
  in my parenting: _____,
  _____, _____,
  _____, and _____.

- My first step toward my parenting intention will be to
  _____.

  (List your parenting goal for this month.)

Write down your parenting intention and keep it somewhere you can refer to it whenever you need to do so. (That might be on your mirror where you can see it every day or maybe in your meditation corner where you can visit it during quiet time.) Just put it somewhere you know you'll read it often.

2

Exploring Childhood Labels

We actually start our parenting journeys way before our children ever take their first breaths. That's because our parenting views begin to take shape in our childhoods; as we see how the adults around us love and care for children, we begin to develop some of our own core beliefs. So many things can influence how we see the parent-child relationship. Unfortunately, as new parents many of us might have been too busy thinking about what we'd name our child or what color to paint the baby's room to consider how our own established beliefs about our own childhoods might eventually show up in our own parenting.

The more I work with families, the more I see that many of us are just full-grown versions of who we were as children. Our bodies and brains grew, but some of our thought patterns, beliefs, and habitual behaviors haven't changed a bit! I like to start at this point when I begin working with families, so let's talk about that inner child for a moment. Many of us walk around with storylines we picked up in our childhoods. And some of us unintentionally repeat the same behaviors that our parents modeled in those storylines. No matter how hard we try, we can't seem to stop turning into our parents! On the other hand, some of us are so afraid of repeating those learned patterns that we choose the complete opposite approach. We avoid parenting like our parents at all costs. Unfortunately, the opposite of unhealthy isn't always healthy! That's especially true in parenting. No worries, though, it's never too late to get curious about your past and right the ship! You can turn the wheel in a different direction whenever you want. In fact, let's do that right now!

Five Common Childhood Storylines

I'm going to outline five of the common childhood labels my clients give themselves. You may see yourself in one of these narratives, or if you grew up with inconsistent parenting you may identify with several. For that reason, I encourage you to read them all, but don't view them as strict interpretations of who you were as a child or who you are as a parent. We are not programmed robots. (I honestly don't even like labels because I know just how complex our individual personalities really are.) Just because you see yourself in one of these examples doesn't mean that you need to own that label. In fact, identifying with one of these examples says more about how you were treated as a child than who you actually are as a person. But by tapping into who you believe you were as a child, you are likely to learn some things about how you're showing up as a parent. As soon as you came into the world, you started adapting to the worldviews of the people around you. These inherited beliefs become the steering wheel for how we parent as adults. And they play a big role in the direction you choose in your own parenting, so they cannot be overlooked. So as you move through these motifs, be honest and stay curious, but also be gentle with yourself.

Take this exercise seriously, but not too seriously, okay? Let it be a reflective practice, but not the absolute truth! I want you to remember that what you believe isn't always the whole story. If you see yourself in these storylines and begin to identify with any of these roles, please know that you can rise above any current thinking and affirm new truths for yourself. (Truer truths, if you will!) We have so much creative power and we can affirm new storylines. After you read through each label, I will ask you some questions about how these beliefs might be showing up in your own life and in your relationship with your child. I won't follow up with what your answers must mean or give you some quick diagnosis; I want you to draw your own conclusions about your answers because *you* are your best teacher. So try not to overanalyze it. In other words, don't call your bestie and start listing everything that's wrong with you or with how you were raised! Chill! There's nothing wrong with you! You just may be walking around with beliefs that don't serve you well, which means you don't need a new you, you just need to adopt a few new beliefs! At the end of each section I provide some affirmations you can use when you feel yourself slipping back into old thought patterns that don't support you and your child. Now, I'm not suggesting that you need to sticky note these affirmations anywhere or say them in the mirror. If that works for you, great, but if not, use them as "in the moment" mantras. (That's what works for me.) When I feel my inner child rising up and panicking, I calm her with affirmations. Yes, I talk to myself, y'all! You don't have to talk to yourself, of course, but I've found it to be very effective for myself, and so have many of my clients.

The Good Child

Would you describe yourself as an "easy" kid? Were you seen and not heard? Did you try your best to stay out of the way? Did you ask for very little? Did you fear disappointing the adults around you? Did you constantly seek approval? Were you regularly praised for your good behavior? Did you receive very few punishments growing up because you rarely made mistakes? I hear many "good child" adults say things like "I got a beating one time and I learned my lesson" or "I never really got into trouble."

A lot of the parents I talk to who grew up like this lean toward perfectionism. They are often really meticulous about not making mistakes and they organize their lives in a way that leaves very little room for error. They are extremely rigid with their boundaries and are hypercritical of themselves. In their relationships, they have very little tolerance for mistakes.

If you resonate with *The Good Child*, consider the following questions:

- How is this experience affecting your relationship with your child?

- How do you respond when your child makes mistakes?

- How are rules made in your house and how are they enforced?

- How do you handle "emotional behaviors" like whining, complaining, and tantrums?

- How comfortable are you with "inconvenient" behaviors like your child not putting on their jacket or them saying something inappropriate at the "wrong" time?

- How do you feel when your child struggles with something like learning a new skill or achieving something?

- Do you struggle with communicating or connecting with your child on a deeper level?

- Do you think your child is a reflection of you and experience shame, embarrassment, or guilt any time they make a mistake?

Asking yourself these questions is a great way to get in touch with how you really want to show up in your parenting. Maybe you see a pattern of perfectionism that you didn't previously see. Growing up having to perform and "be good" is a lot of pressure. If you were *The Good Child*, you probably had expectations that were way beyond your actual development. You may have learned that "being good" was the only way to gain acceptance and safety in your environment.

You may have learned that children having big feelings, big needs, or big problems was inconvenient.

Now, this is not to say that some children don't have a generally agreeable temperament. But if you were not comfortable making mistakes or being curious in your environment, then you didn't really get the opportunity to explore who you are outside of who your caretakers wanted you to be. So in the parent-child relationship, consider if you do actually want your child to grow into the truest version of themself. If so, you can shift from perfectionism. You can invite more flexibility into your home. You can begin intentionally teaching your child that mistakes are a normal, natural part of learning and growing.

Here's an example of what that shift can look like. A client of mine was having a really difficult time connecting with her son. (We'll call her "Pam.") Pam attributed their lack of connection to their differing personalities. She was very extroverted. She enjoyed socializing and spent a lot of time in her community. Her son (we'll call him "James") was the complete opposite. He liked to keep to himself and spent much of his time in his room. Having different temperaments definitely can make it difficult to connect in relationships; however, as we explored her situation further I began to see that the root of the disconnect probably wasn't their different personalities at all. As we kept talking, Pam began raving about how great a kid her son was. She explained that he never gave her a hard time and always did what she asked. She was really proud of the fact that she didn't have to discipline him and that he was so easy! She said that she held him to a really high standard and was very hard on him. There were a lot of rules in her house and though she never spanked or yelled, she spent an unreasonable amount of time lecturing James on her expectations.

Pam grew up in a similar environment where the expectations were very clear and very high. She was quite proud of this. She attributed a lot of her success to the way her parents molded her. So I started asking Pam questions about how she felt about making mistakes, failing, and growth. She admitted that she carried that same pressure from her childhood into adulthood. She realized that she was hard on James because she was hard on herself. As a result, Pam began noticing that James was also getting increasingly harder on himself. She first noticed this when he started to struggle with his homework. He had a really hard time coping with not getting things "right." This is when she started to notice the disconnect between them. She would try to encourage him, but the more she encouraged him, the more he shut down. He rarely wanted to talk about his struggles and had a difficult time asking her for help. He would power through his homework and then just go to bed on most days. She was proud of his perseverance but something felt off. She felt like his light was dimming and he was generally sadder than usual. She wanted to help him but she realized that she had not created an environment where he felt safe being imperfect around her.

So rather than focusing on their personalities or suggesting fun activities to do together, I invited her to first begin noticing when she was leaning into perfectionism in her own life. I told her, "If modeling perfectionism got you here, modeling grace and acceptance can get you somewhere else." And so she began just noticing when she was putting too much pressure on herself. She came up with the following affirmation: "I'm trying to be perfect. But I'm not perfect. And I don't want to be perfect. I want to be me." And in those moments when she missed the deadline or couldn't find the perfect photo to post on Instagram, she started using that mantra to remind herself of the new beliefs that she was trying to adopt. She also started leaning on her husband more for help. Rather than powering through daily tasks and getting overwhelmed, she began simply saying, "I need help." She found it really funny that her husband was completely shocked the first time he heard her say this, but she reminded him of her commitment to modeling healthy expectations of herself, and together they began to reinforce new behaviors in their home. Ironically, her relationship with James wasn't "perfect," even after these changes. However, they grew much closer without the pressure of having to always get it "right." Had we skipped over Pam's very real need to heal her own perfectionism, the changes in their relationship likely wouldn't have lasted.

If you are struggling with perfectionism, I invite you to make a commitment to yourself and to your family to start adopting new, less unrealistic expectations. This is simply about noticing the patterns. You are not broken. There is nothing to fix. But when we become aware of our patterns, we make subtle shifts toward compassion and grace for ourselves and our families. This is your opportunity to create something new.

Affirmations for *The Good Child*

- I can make mistakes. They don't define me. My mistakes help me grow.

- I forgive myself. I am allowed to mess up.

- I don't have all the answers, and that's okay.

- My kids don't need me to be perfect.

- I can handle my child's big feelings.

- I can support my child when they make mistakes.

- My needs matter. I can ask for what I need.

- My child's needs matter. They can ask for what they need.

- I can set fair boundaries with my children.

- I have everything I need inside me. I don't need approval or validation.

- I am enough.

- I love my child for who they are.

- I value connection over perfection.
- My flaws don't make me unworthy.
- Progress, not perfection.
- When my child needs me, I am here to help.
- It's okay to ask for help.
- We share this space. No one's needs are more important than the others.
- We are all safe, loved, and seen.

The Bad Child

Maybe you were always getting into trouble. Did you hear your parents talk about you like you were a burden? Were you constantly compared to a sibling or other kids? Did your parents notice more negative things about you than positive? Were you punished harshly? Did you learn to expect spankings, yelling, or criticism regularly? These parents often say things like "I got spanked all the time" or "I was a handful!"

Unlike *The Good Child*, you may have experienced a lot of punishments. As a result, you might be extremely reactive in your relationships. Because patience, emotional regulation, and healthy discipline were not modeled, you may lean toward shaming, blaming, and punishing. If you're uncomfortable with your own unfavorable behavior, it may be difficult for you to navigate conflict when your child struggles with their own.

If you resonate with *The Bad Child*, consider the following questions:

- How do you think this experience shows up in your parenting?
- Do you use punishments (yelling, taking things, spankings, timeouts) as a form of discipline?

- Do you find yourself using blaming language like "This is your fault" or "See what happens when you don't listen?"

- How do you react when your child says something you don't agree with? Do you quickly jump to correct them or are you able to explore their opinions more?

- Do you use shaming language like "You are bad, mean, evil, rude, a jerk, etc."?

- Are you easily triggered by your child's mistakes?

- How easy is it for you to calm down when you are triggered?

- Do you find yourself punishing, shaming, and blaming yourself?

The Bad Child didn't have emotional safety. They experienced very reactive parenting and as a result were in a constant state of insecurity. And that insecurity can often manifest in impulse parenting. As parents, they may struggle to create secure and consistent environments for their children. And because their boundaries were not respected when they were children, they can find it very difficult to create their own boundaries and also respect the boundaries of others. They may perpetuate reactiveness and struggle to find rational responses to the unfavorable behaviors of their children.

When I work with these parents, they often have a strong desire to change. They want to be more responsive and less reactive. They want to be fair and honor and respect their children, but they often can find it really difficult to do. Constantly receiving negative attention for years as children can result in strongly rooted shame stories, which can make it very difficult to make changes in their parenting roles. It can be helpful for *The Bad Child* to start their journey by practicing self-forgiveness and acceptance. (You have to deal with the belief before you can deal with the behaviors.)

For many who identify with *The Bad Child*, there is a belief that they don't deserve forgiveness, acceptance, or grace. So we start with learning these skills before we begin to focus on the yelling or punishing!

Now I was the "bad child" for sure. After a while, I completely adapted to the role and I became mischievous for sport. I thought, "Hey, I'm probably gonna f*ck up today anyway. I might as well make it a show!" But the more I gave in to that belief, the more trouble I got into. And the more trouble I got into, the harder it was for the adults around to love me. And that cycle created my shame story. As an adult do you think I just dropped the narrative? No! In my head, I went from a bad kid to a bad woman to a bad mom. And that is a "shame story" I have to unpack and notice every single day. Sometimes I can silence that voice completely and have an amazing day. Other times, I can get it down to a whisper and I just do my best. And still there are times where the "shame story" screams my inadequacies at me. The difference now is that I'm no longer being totally controlled by the belief. I can experience it for the moment but still recognize that it's not rooted in fact. As one of my favorite coaches, Preston Smiles, would say: it's not actually true with a capital "T." I can recognize that as true. *The Bad Child* narrative might seem true in the moment, but it's not the *Truth* and it's not the whole picture. And that leaves space for me to affirm more productive beliefs about myself.

Here's what shifting may look like for someone who, like me, has the "bad child" belief. Let's say you've had a challenging day. You know, one of those days where you didn't get enough sleep the night before and you snapped at the kids for something small and your boss had to talk to you about your performance and you also burned dinner! And when you finally sit down to your glass of wine and charred dinner you realize you forgot your best friend's birthday was that same day. You fought off the shame story all day, but this was the last straw! You can't hold it back and the tears and the thoughts come flooding uncontrollably.

2 Exploring Childhood Labels

"I'm a terrible mom."

"I can't stop snapping."

"I suck at this."

"What kind of person forgets their best friend's birthday?"

You feel all the feelings. But then, because you've accepted that this is a belief you're working on, you begin to consciously notice it.

"Ah, I'm doing the 'bad child' thing again. It feels really true this time. And I'm having a hard time not believing it. I wonder if there's any evidence that it's not capital 'T' true. Could I start with just one thing that proves I don't suck?"

Then you remember that you cooked breakfast for the first time in two weeks today. And you remind yourself of the moment you hugged your toddler for absolutely no reason. And you were such a great listener when your oldest needed to vent. (And you didn't interrupt her once.) And you then choose some positive affirmations for the moment like "I'm allowed to make mistakes" or "I forgive myself." And then, once you've calmed your storm, you remember how amazing your best friend is and how understanding she'll be if you just call her now. You were able to shift and remember that you are doing a good job at many things and you are not "the bad child" or "the bad mom."

Affirmations for *The Bad Child*

- I forgive myself.
- I am allowed to make mistakes.
- I am enough.
- I am loved and supported.
- I have compassion for myself and others.
- I can calm myself when I am triggered.

- I am learning to love myself, one day at a time.
- I love my child.
- When my child makes a mistake, they need more love, not less.
- My child is enough.
- I can handle my child's behavior calmly and fairly.
- I am the right parent for my child.
- I'm doing a great job with the tools that I have.
- I am learning to be kinder to myself every single day.
- I can respect my boundaries and the boundaries of others.
- I freely give and receive love.
- I am worthy and valuable.

The Golden Child

Maybe you could do no wrong growing up! Did your parents make excuses for your behavior? Did they bail you out every time you had a conflict? Did they give you very little discipline? Did they exaggerate your strengths and accomplishments while ignoring your weaknesses? Did they consistently step in and save you even when you were more than capable of doing something on your own? These parents often say things like "My parents did everything for me" or "I was their favorite child."

These clients often struggle with creating fair and balanced relationships. They typically find themselves in unbalanced dynamics where there is a clear taker and a clear giver. Sometimes they perpetuate their role in childhood and only focus on getting their needs met. Other times, they re-create the role of their parents and give all of their energy, resources, and time to meeting their child's needs while they neglect their own. Because they rarely had to be responsible as a child, they may also struggle with accountability and personal responsibility. They either have a difficult time owning their choices and dealing with consequences or they have a hard time holding their children accountable. This makes creating a fair environment a challenge.

If you resonate with *The Golden Child*, consider the following questions:

- How is this experience impacting your parenting?

- How much input does your child have on your home environment?

- How often do you say "yes" when you really want to say "no"?

- How often do you say "no" when you could have said "yes"?

- Is your relationship with your child balanced?

- Are you intentional about making sure that everyone's needs get met?

- How do you respond when you are unfair with your child? Are you able to recognize it and take accountability?

- How do you respond to your child's inappropriate behavior? Are you able to hold them accountable?

- Do you have a difficult time keeping promises or commitments with your child?

- Do you have a difficult time keeping promises or commitments with yourself?

A starting goal for *The Golden Child* may be to focus on creating accountability and balance in their relationships. Because we start with personal responsibility, these parents may want to start noticing how they show up in other relationships and noticing times when they are being either too rigid or too loose with their boundaries. They can pay more attention to how they take accountability for their actions.

I've worked with a mother whose parents rarely held her accountable. She grew up having very little personal responsibility. She said her parents did everything for her—from her homework to filling out job applications. And whenever she got in trouble at school, her parents "handled it." She knew she wanted to raise her children differently, so we got to work and began the process of setting clear boundaries within her family relationships. She went through the process of creating boundaries. She was really excited that she was creating a more intentional environment, but still nothing seemed to change. It was as if the boundaries only mattered to her. She stated, "We all agreed to take on more responsibility around the house—even my husband—but when it's actually time to clean, no one lifts a finger." So I asked her what her response to this behavior was and that's when the manifestation of *The Golden Child* emerged. She said she would get so frustrated that she ended up just cleaning up the entire house herself. Because she was not taught the importance of being held accountable, she had a really hard time maintaining limits with her children. This was creating resentment because the less her children contributed, the more responsibility she took on. She was carrying the weight of the responsibility in the house when she could have shared it with her children and her husband.

The current vibe in the house was extremely unbalanced. She had unintentionally nurtured a very unbalanced relationship with her family. So we decided to take a step back from what was happening in the home and start looking at other areas of her life where she could start practicing the process of creating balance. I began teaching her how to clearly articulate her needs and her boundaries in her friendships and other adult relationships. It was also clear that she also needed to work on respecting others' boundaries. By working on new, empowering language, she began to create much more equity in her relationships where there was no clear giver or taker. Rather, everyone's needs were acknowledged and met. She learned how to voice her expectations and express her limits in her relationships. She learned to clearly articulate when her boundaries were crossed. She started holding people accountable... including herself.

Affirmations for *The Golden Child*

- I take responsibility for my life, my decisions, and my choices.

- My mistakes don't make me unworthy. They make me human.

- Boundaries are valuable and help me connect more deeply with others.

- Everyone gets to be seen, loved, and appreciated in my home.

- I can set clear expectations. I can hold my boundaries.

- I respect the boundaries that others set.

- "No" is a complete sentence.

- I am responsible for my energy.

- I am capable of finding solutions to my problems.

- I don't need to be saved.

- It's okay to ask for help, but I can do many things on my own.

- My children can do hard things.

- I can do hard things.

- I value a growth mindset. When I take accountability, I grow.

- It is my responsibility to repair and make amends when I have misused, disrespected, or hurt someone... even my children.

- I lovingly hold my children accountable when they make mistakes.

The Black Sheep

Did you feel like there was no way you were related to the people in your house? Did you prefer being by yourself? Did your parents have a difficult time connecting with you or celebrating your differences? Did you feel misunderstood or not "seen"? Did your parents call you names like "oddball" or "weirdo"? Did you find yourself disagreeing with your parents often?

When my clients describe themselves as the black sheep in their families, they often feel very burdened. They express a lot of loneliness and a struggle to make genuine connections in relationships. They have a hard time trusting that they are safe to be seen. If they have not yet found spaces where they feel comfortable in their own skin, they may pass their insecurities on to their children. Growing up in an environment where differences aren't celebrated can make it difficult for *The Black Sheep* to connect and be vulnerable with their children. I also see a lot of isolation in these clients. They don't typically seek out community and tend to keep to themselves. As parents, they might avoid extracurriculars, play dates, and recreational activities. They don't tend to have a lot of strong relationships outside of their families and thus don't have as much support as they might otherwise.

If you resonated with *The Black Sheep*, consider the following questions:

- How is this experience showing up in your parenting?

- Do you feel seen, loved, and supported for who you are?

- In what ways do you celebrate your child's differences?
- Are you uncomfortable with any elements of your child's personality?
- Are you uncomfortable with any elements of your own personality?
- How do you deal with that discomfort?
- How do you support your child in making friends and connecting with others?
- How often do you have deeper, more intimate conversations with your child?
- How would you describe your community involvement?
- If you don't have a strong connection to a community, why do you think that is?
- Is it easy or difficult for you to make friends and connect with other adults?

A huge theme in *The Black Sheep*'s childhood is judgment. Parents who relate to *The Black Sheep* often isolate themselves because they fear the same rejection they experienced in childhood. With that said, it's damn near impossible to grow up in a hypercritical environment and not develop judgmental habits yourself. I'm a self-proclaimed black sheep in my family, and it can be very lonely. For a long time, I hated being around people! That sounds crazy to me now, but it was my truth for much of my parenting journey. I hated family functions. And you wouldn't catch me at a playdate. And this behavior was absolutely two-sided: I feared being judged but I also judged every little thing about others. Any time I was around my family, I was on edge: "God. Did my kid just break something? They probably think I'm the worst parent ever." But I also couldn't help judging them right back. The same was true at playdates. I felt like I was performing rather than connecting, so I just stopped participating altogether. I shut out the world for a while. But isolation makes parenting even more challenging. And worse, I was teaching my children this behavior. I knew something had to change. Of course, I wasn't just going to force myself into spaces that didn't resonate with me or feel appropriate. But I got very intentional about finding friends and community that I felt comfortable with. I've learned over the years that I don't have to block the world out to feel safe. There are spaces where I can be uniquely myself. And the more comfortable I get in creating community, the more I see my children blossom and appreciate their own uniqueness. This is still quite difficult for me and there may always be a part of me that gives people the side eye and struggles to trust that I'm not being judged, but I combat that moment by moment with my affirmation practice.

Affirmations for *The Black Sheep*

- I trust myself a little more day by day.

- I am releasing my fear of rejection.

- I can find my tribe. There are people willing to support me.

- I am attracting friends and family that will accept me just the way I am.

- My children are safe with me.

- I can find other safe spaces for my children.

- I am learning to forgive people who have judged me incorrectly.

- I do not need anyone's approval or acceptance to be whole.

- I go where I am celebrated, not tolerated.

- I celebrate myself. I celebrate my children.

- I am learning to love myself unconditionally.

- I'm so grateful for who I am.

- I don't have to do this alone. I can create community and attract supportive friends and family.

- I accept those around me and release judgment.

- There is so much abundance around me.

- I am learning to be comfortable in my skin in every room I enter.

The Independent Child

Were you "adulting" quite young? Did you take on a lot of responsibility, and were you praised for being so independent? Did people describe you as "wise beyond your years"? Were you hypersensitive to the needs of those around you? Did you have to be the caretaker for other siblings or even your parents? I often hear these parents say things like "I grew up fast" or "I didn't really have a childhood."

If you believe you were *The Independent Child*, you may unintentionally place this same responsibility on your child. This can especially be true if that unhealthy independence just rolled over into adulthood. If you rarely ask for help and take on unrealistic responsibilities outside of parenting, you may not have as much time to meet your child's needs. So they may also be consistently put in situations where they have to fend for themselves.

If you can relate to *The Independent Child*, ask yourself these questions:

- How does this experience show up in your parenting?

- How much intentional, intimate time do you spend with your child?

- Would you consider yourself overworked, chronically busy, or burned out?

- Do your friends and family praise you for being able to "get so much done"?

- How easy is it to get help or support if you need it?

- How do you respond when your child needs help with a simple task?

- How do you respond when your child needs help with a difficult task?

- Do you struggle to fully understand your child's needs?

- How do you practice self-care?

The Independent Child learned very quickly how to meet everyone else's needs. This is a recipe for poor boundaries. Having to constantly ignore your own boundaries, you may not have learned how to say "no" or how to ask for help. While *The Independent Child* learns how to *do,* they don't necessarily learn how to just *be.* They weren't taught how to sit with their needs and their experience because they were constantly bombarded with the requests and expectations of others. Being parentified and having to speed up mental maturity does not mean that *The Independent Child* also matures emotionally. As adults, these parents often take on so much responsibility, but they hit emotional walls extremely hard when they can't keep up.

It can be a heavy burden to feel like you have to do everything for your child and give them the best. My clients who identify with *The Independent Child* story feel this burden extremely heavily. They often work extremely hard, prioritize order and keeping things together, and put important things like connection, self-care, and intimacy on the back burner. Because of this, creating emotional safety and lowering the productivity expectations is really helpful for these clients.

I think of my own mother. She was such an incredible mom. If I had to attribute where I am in life to one person it would undoubtedly be her. She was my best friend. Before she passed we talked every single day, multiple times a day. I crack up when I hear parents asking for help with a co-sleeping toddler because I was snuggling up in my mom's bed every time I visited her, even as an adult. I never felt more accepted by a human than I did when I was with her. But it wasn't always that way. Growing up, I had a lot of behavioral issues and we bumped heads frequently. She did everything for me. This woman always had five billion jobs at one time just to make sure that I had everything I needed and wanted. But because she worked so hard to take care of us, we rarely had time to connect.

As I got older, I realized how much of a burden my mom's independence was on her. If my mom were here today, I would tell her to release the pressure she was putting on herself. I would have stopped spending so much time trying to get her to connect with me and encouraged her to make time to connect with herself.

That is where I start with *The Independent Child*. Yes, you have bills and obligations, and a healthy dose of hustle and independence, but how can you also start to have more intimacy, connection, and compassion with yourself? What are you prioritizing that isn't actually more of a priority than your well-being? Positive, connected relationships will flow from your ability to give yourself some grace. You can't show up as a more compassionate, available parent if you don't first do that for yourself.

Affirmations for *The Independent Child*

- Right now, my child needs my help.

- I need help. And that is okay.

- I can say "no" to things that do not serve my well-being.

- Right now I am fully present. I have nowhere I *need* to go and nothing I *need* to do.

- I can sit with my breath for a few moments.
- I am here to support my child.
- Every single day I will do something to prioritize myself.
- Today, I will carve out intentional time to connect.
- I don't have to do this alone.
- I am supported.
- I don't have to feel shame when I say "no."
- I deserve my free time. Self-care is not selfish.
- I know how to say what I need. And right now I need
  _____.

A Closing Thought

If you are struggling to find harmony in your home, it may be because the scales were likely not balanced in your childhood. And now you might find yourself repeating a one-sided dynamic where children are expected to give more than they are developmentally capable. Or you may have created the opposite, yet still one-sided space where you are expected to give more than you are capable. But everybody deserves to have their needs met. And that is possible. You don't have to live in the "Or" space where one of you has to suffer while the other wins. You can live in the "And" space, instead. You can set limits *and* give compassion. You can see your child as good *and* still recognize and coach them through their mistakes. You can help your child *and* still foster their independence.

While we all have these stories and experiences, I hope this exercise has started you on the journey of liberation from beliefs that don't serve you. I hope, rather than you wearing any of these labels, you will see this as an opportunity to tell your own story and create more balance for your family. As you read on, you will have the opportunity to create beliefs that support your family so that you can drop the labels and parent with more presence and intention.

3

Becoming the Parent You Needed

When we take ownership of our lives, anything is possible. I am rooted in this belief. Unfortunately, many of us are stripped of our power in our childhoods. This is evident in the false labels some of us walk around with. So, before you make any positive changes in your relationship with your child, you have to start with your relationship to the first child you ever knew—your inner child.

Reparenting the Parent

Now don't run away if this seems a bit scary. I'm not suggesting we unpack every single childhood memory. You do that in therapy! I'm only interested in your childhood to the extent that we can figure out what you didn't receive in the past so you can begin giving yourself those things in the present. This process is called *reparenting*. Reparenting puts you in an empowered stance. Rather than looking for a savior or blaming your parents for your missing pieces, you can learn to lean into your own capabilities to raise yourself. And through this process, you can become hopeful, understanding that it's never too late to give yourself whatever it is you need. Through reparenting, you can look at the level of love, the amount of security, and the type of discipline you might have needed to thrive as a child. And then you can commit to giving yourself those things.

You know why this is so powerful? When you give yourself more love, security, and discipline, your capacity to give your children the same things will expand. As a coach, I have found that the most powerful shifts in the family dynamic really start with the parents understanding their needs and what they did not receive in their childhoods, and then turning that into an intentional journey where they first parent themselves so that they can show up as better parents for their own children.

Where Do You Start?

So how do you do this? How do you "show up" for yourself to fulfill these unmet needs? Unfortunately, I can't answer that question for you. Only you can. The reparenting journey will look different for all of us. Your inner child does not need what my inner child needs, so I can't give you the exact right tools for what you need. Just like a conscious parent, you know yourself best. And it is my hope that through this journey you'll get to know yourself even better. So I can't offer the done-for-you guide to reparenting. Nope! But what I can offer you is some intentional shifts in the way you approach yourself so that reparenting will flow naturally. We are human beings, not human doings! I don't just want to teach you *what to do*. I want to offer you some mindset shifts that can guide you on *how to be*. I believe that it's only when we are intentional about our *being* that we are able to make effective use of the tools we learn. And here's the bonus: when you get more rooted in how to be and show up for yourself, you begin to strengthen your own inner guidance system so that you can create and access your own tools. There's no better feeling than not having to jump onto Google to find out what to do in every single situation with your child. Some of us are so disconnected from our own needs that we are completely at a loss when it comes to our children's needs.

It's time to feel more confident in your choices as a parent. It's time to step away from the toolkit for a second and strengthen your inner guidance system.

The Reparenting Shifts

In each of the following sections, I will introduce a shift and invite you to consider what that shift might look like for you specifically. I will provide examples, prompts, and even affirmations. However, this is only meant to serve as a starting point for you to explore which tools will align with you. As you move through each shift, please remember this: you do not need fixing. It is the cycles that need repair, not you. Like my therapist once told me, you are taking care of a garden full of seeds you did not plant. So be intentional, but go easy on yourself through this process. Let's get started!

Shift: Awareness

The very first shift you can make in your reparenting journey is an intentional shift in your awareness. As you reparent yourself, you get to give yourself more love through your ability to see through different eyes. Now, the culture that we live in does not often allow for much consciousness; a lot of us grew up in environments where the adults around us were not very aware of the implications of their actions. So many of our parents modeled autopilot living where they adapted to their environments without questioning why they did so. They did this because that is what was modeled for them. This is a common aspect of the current human condition— especially in Western culture. We fall into the beliefs and patterns of those around us and we adopt them without question. We learn to ignore our inner voices and start reacting to situations based on conditioning. Very early on in life you may have received the message that you should constantly be adapting to your environment. If we wanted to keep up or be accepted as we grew up, we had to turn our own innate senses off and conform to the world around us. We all experienced this to a certain extent, even in the most flexible households.

I know this is true of my own personal experience. And though my parents never put it into words, this is what I learned as soon as I could comprehend: "No matter what, if X, then Y." If you talked back, you were bad. If you didn't make your bed, you were lazy. If an adult didn't like something, you didn't do it. To make matters worse, every system I moved through had its own set of "if–then" rules. In school, if you didn't wear this and talk like that, you wouldn't fit in. In church, if you weren't this religion, you weren't righteous, good, or worthy. In public, if you didn't speak to the lady at the cash register, you were being rude. All these rules! My parents and the people around me gave them to me to keep me safe. They wanted to protect me from the things they feared. I deeply understand that now and have no resentment toward the messages I received in my childhood. Still, life as an adult is a constant journey of recognizing whether an internalized belief is helpful or harmful in the present. Maybe some of the same rules and beliefs served you well in previous environments, but something greater is calling you. The further you move away from who you really are, the less aligned you feel. It's that dis-ease that rests above your thoughts every day. You can't quite put your finger on it. You just know that you're here for something better than your current patterns and habits. This is where your awareness comes in. When you commit to questioning your existing thought patterns and behaviors, you examine your current beliefs. Begin by asking yourself where each thought comes from. What do you truly value? Why is something a pet peeve? What do you need to learn in order to expand? You *can* become a student again. But this time you're in charge of the curriculum. You get to be curious again, like when you were a child, exploring yourself and the world around you. Rather than flowing with your environment, you get to become a master of it.

In order to begin this process, I've created some journal prompts to help you increase your awareness. As you answer them, I hope you learn a bit more about yourself. The more you practice answering these kinds of questions, the better you'll become at hearing, understanding, and honoring your own inner voice:

- What do you love about yourself?
- Where did you learn that these were favorable characteristics?
- What are your least favorite things about yourself?
- Why do you think these are unfavorable characteristics?
- What are you afraid of? Where do those fears come from?
- What are things you do because you enjoy them?
- What are things you do out of obligation and not because you enjoy them?
- What decisions are you currently making in your life out of fear?
- What relationships do you currently maintain out of obligation?
- What relationships do you currently maintain out of love?

Imagine a loving parent enthusiastically encouraging such curiosity in their child. By exploring these prompts and asking yourself these questions, you can be that loving parent to yourself. It is only through curiosity that we learn who we really are without the rules, labels, and beliefs. So we start our reparenting process here—in the space of awareness and curiosity.

Think back to being a child. Think of the hours you could spend with the most trivial task. In youth, time stands still as children dig holes in the dirt or inquisitively flick those springy door stoppers!

As we reparent, we get to return to the openness and expansiveness that we had in our minds before the adults came in with their own fears and projections. We can see things through a different lens. Children don't see problems that need fixing; they see parts of themselves and their worlds that need exploring.

Can you look at your day-to-day experiences with more curiosity? Can you start questioning your knee-jerk reactions, your preferences, and your desires? Can you look at your habits and beliefs and just get curious about them? This is called *witnessing*. We can't physically step out of our bodies, but we can take notice of our thoughts and behaviors. We can approach ourselves the way we approached those holes and door stoppers!

Shift: Nonjudgment

As you become more aware of your environment and begin seeing the world more curiously, you may find yourself wanting to analyze and judge what you find. This is especially true when we discover things from our past and present that feel uncomfortable or evoke strong emotional responses. At this point, you might find yourself saying things like "Yikes! I'm doing that thing that my mom used to do. No wonder my kid resents me" or "I should be less afraid of failure. It's holding me back." And that's awesome that you're noticing things more clearly. But don't let that be an invitation to create stories around your experiences. Instead, let an increase in your awareness also be an opportunity for you to increase your level of acceptance and nonjudgment.

The idea of nonjudgment is really summed up in a phrase my mom always used to say to me: "It is what it is." Pretty simple, I know. And at first glance it can seem a little lazy. It sounds a bit complacent, right? For a long time I just dismissed the phrase as an unproductive thing people say when they don't want things to change. That is until I shifted my level of acceptance. That's when the phrase became a powerful tool in coping with my negative thought patterns. The other side of the phrase "It is what it is" is "It isn't what it isn't." And that's where you find your power. When you can describe a negative experience in the plainest terms, it loses its grip on you. When you can express your grievances or frustrations without any added narratives or assumptions, you leave room for positive change. "It is what it is" is the mantra that reminds me to simply make observations about my experiences. This allows me to accept the things I cannot change and find constructive solutions for the things that are within my control. It may be different next week. It may be different thirty seconds from now, but right now, in this moment, it is what it is. Nothing more and nothing less. Here are some examples of how I often put this simple phrase to work:

"A diagnosis? It's just a diagnosis. It doesn't have to define me."

"My past? It's just my past. It doesn't mean I can't create something new."

"A tough day of parenting? It's just a tough day of parenting. It doesn't mean I suck."

These are simple examples, but how often do we take our experiences and attach to them some grand story about what could have happened or what happens next? What I'm describing here is *rumination*. It's that negative loop that plays when you're struggling to accept things. It's the should-haves, could-haves, and would-haves we assign to the past and the catastrophic outcomes we assign to the future. It's the story we tell ourselves, and it's often disproportionately focused on the negative. And it's here for many of us because of our childhood experiences. Did you grow up in a highly reactive or frantic environment where uncomfortable experiences and feelings felt like emergencies? This could have looked like your parents being extremely reactive with your big emotions and behaviors. Conversely, they may have been completely unavailable for your big emotions and behaviors, leaving you to process those experiences on your own. And so you may be living in this constant state of overarousal that makes it difficult for you to just sit with an experience or feeling.

As an example of rumination, I spent most of my divorce dwelling on the past and catastrophizing the future. I would think: "Oh my gosh, why did I even get married? This is the end of the world. My child is going to grow up in a terrible environment. She'll be scarred for life and I'm never going to find love again." I had so many stories that were keeping me from actually getting through my present experience of going through a divorce.

Though these stories are not the only things controlling your well-being, they do play a huge part. We often move toward the things we focus on, whether they are helpful or harmful. Rumination can cause you to self-sabotage because your limiting beliefs about the past and your negative expectations of the future will directly impact your behaviors. And those behaviors become the sum of your experience. This is why acceptance is so important. When we focus on the past, we sink into shame and sometimes even depression. When we focus on the future, we open ourselves up to constant anxiety. But acceptance in the present gives you clarity to find solutions without the added stress of judgment. The following journal prompts will help you explore the areas of your life that need less judgment:

- What situations in the present are you struggling to accept? What judgments are you adding to these situations?

- What experiences from the past are you holding on to? What judgments are you adding to these experiences? What stories about the future are you rehearsing that you need to release? (I am telling myself _____.)

- How are these things impacting your behavior? (My judgments about the past, present, and future are causing me to _____.)

Shift: Presence

Many of us grew up in environments where the adults around us were not present. Some of us had parents operating in survival mode and they quite literally didn't have the time or the emotional or mental capacities to be present. Others grew up in homes where presence just wasn't prioritized. Maybe there wasn't much space for play in your home. Maybe no one stopped to get curious about you and your day on a consistent basis. Maybe you didn't feel seen. I don't want you to get too hung up on the specifics—it really isn't necessary for the reparenting process—all you need to know is what you missed out on, and for many of us that was attention and presence. So here you are, years later, with an opportunity to give yourself the level of attuned attention that you need and deserve.

When I look back at my experiences, there were many times when I did not feel seen or understood. I was definitely labeled the black sheep and the bad kid in my family, and I played both roles extremely well. (Cue the self-destructive behaviors!) I tried so many inappropriate ways to feel seen because I was desperate for the attention and intimacy I was missing. It has taken a very long time, lots of failed relationships, and tons of therapy to recognize that I can see, love, and accept myself by giving myself more intentional attention. When people feel seen, they soar! And so if we want to soar in our parenting or any area of our lives, for that matter, we have to find healthy ways to be seen on a consistent basis.

Anytime I say the word "presence" to myself, it's like a cue or a trigger for me to be still. A deep breath, conscious awareness of my thoughts, and active engagement with my environment are all ways that I reparent myself through more presence. (And if you haven't taken a deep breath all day, well, here's your invitation.) Now, this could be easier said than done for some of us. Remember that highly reactive, frantic environment I was talking about some of us growing up in earlier? That type of experience can literally change your brain, causing your nervous system to constantly communicate a threat response to your body even when there isn't a threat present. This makes tasks like sitting quietly with yourself a bit uncomfortable. So if presence is new for you, it may be hard to convince yourself to power through something so uncomfortable, especially on a consistent basis. It makes sense; you can't just change your physiology overnight. And I'm not asking you to work against your current capacity. Maybe you don't have five minutes for a breathwork meditation. (I mean, let's be honest, you probably do if you try.) But for some of us that just feels gravely impossible. No worries. I'd rather look at the moments where you have already carved time out of your day. Let's think about those autopilot tasks that you really don't need to think much about to complete. Moments like self-care and hygiene routines, driving, cooking, housework, lying in bed before you to go to sleep. These are typically moments where our minds are on everything except the present! But these are all opportunities to get more conscious and invite a little more presence into our days. I like to take these moments to do grounding exercises. These exercises have had an incredible impact on my reactivity. The more I return to calm throughout my day, the easier it is to access that calm when I'm triggered. So when people ask how I'm so patient with my children, it's because I practice these exercises when my kids aren't triggering me. Don't wait until the shit hits the fan to learn to be calm—practice it consistently throughout the day.

I want you to think about those unconscious moments in your day when are you on autopilot mode doing mundane tasks or routine activities. In those moments, I want to invite you to try this quick practice:

1. Take three deep breaths.

2. Notice three simple things in your environment. (This could be as simple as the way the steering wheel feels in your hands or the ticking of the clock on the wall.)

3. Ask yourself: "How do I feel?" (Resist the urge to add a "because;" just practice naming your feelings.)

4. Take one more *really* deep breath.

5. Thank yourself for the moment of presence.

6. Carry on with your day!

Shift: Energy

As you invite more presence into your day, you must also become more aware of your energy. Are you treating yourself like a gift or a burden? Are you moving through your coping tools with force or with ease? Are you speaking to yourself with kindness or animosity? The energy we give ourselves paves the way for the energy we give our children. Making an intentional effort to give ourselves whatever energy we need in the moment is a powerful game changer!

Think back to the adults in your childhood for a moment. What was their energy like when they interacted with you? Did they seem excited, calm, exuberant, or joyful? Or did they seem drained, irritated, anxious, or rushed? As the "bad child" growing up, I experienced a lot of the latter. For starters, I was genuinely much harder to parent than my sibling. I can't deny it! This must have been extremely difficult for my parents, who didn't subscribe to the same intentional tools outlined in this book. I'm not giving them a "pass" and it isn't my fault, but trust me, I wasn't an easy child. Considering how much energy my parents had to expend to parent me it's no surprise they were often irritated and annoyed by my presence. And because their energetic cups weren't full, I'm sure the general vibe was "I just busted my butt all day to provide for you. I am exhausted. Just clean your damn room!" And I felt that energy. And more than any of their specific behaviors, I remember how I felt around my parents, in return. Like them, I was constantly irritated and annoyed. And if I'm not careful, I can fall back into this same energy with my own children. That's why it's important for me to first regulate the energy I give to myself. This is a part of the reparenting process.

Maybe your parents showed up to their role with empty cups or heavy hearts, so you were consistently met with annoyance and irritation or anger and frustration. Maybe you adopted some of this energy and began to feel like a burden, even in moments that should have been playful or intimate. If this resonates with you, you need to know that you can shift this for yourself now. As you re-parent, you get to rewrite that story by interacting with yourself in a more energy focused way.

As you go through your daily routine, be conscious of how you show up for yourself. In the beginning, it may be easiest to practice having intentional positive energy toward yourself when accessing reparenting tools, using coping skills, or spending time alone. During your self-talk practice, exercise, self-care, breathwork, and meditation, you have a choice to either power through them or delight in them! You can choose to be kind to yourself! It's one thing to robotically regurgitate positive self-talk. It's another thing to truly celebrate yourself. Consider the ways you can delight in yourself with the kind of energy you wish you had received in your childhood. Can you bring more consciousness into your shower or your skin care routine and find something to celebrate about your body and all that it does for you? Can you coach yourself through tough moments the way you would a struggling friend? Can you put an extra pep in your step on your morning walk? Can you treat yourself to your favorite things sometimes? Can you practice your affirmations in a more organic way? I love the idea of giving yourself a high-five, as Mel Robbins outlines in her book *The High Five Habit*. The basic premise is that when you high-five yourself in the mirror, you activate the same positive programming that you feel when someone else high-fives or encourages you. And let me say it's one of the weirdest, yet oddly satisfying parts of my day! And while some of these ideas may feel "cheesy" or don't quite resonate with you, I know there are ways you can be kinder to yourself. (Honestly, a good old-fashioned nap is the ultimate in self-kindness for me!)

This kind of energetic shift can feel awkward at first. We are not often taught to delight in ourselves. There's so much focus on responsibility and structure. But what if, over time, we were slowly being stripped of one of the most healing characteristics— our joyfulness? It's time to get it back. So when it feels strange, I encourage you to let it be strange. Looking at yourself in the mirror and saying "Damn girl, you look amazing" might feel weird, but it's weird because it's new, not because it's untrue. When I started taking dance class it felt odd. But it was odd because it was new, not because it was a waste of time. So whatever brings you joy and makes you feel encouraged, keep at it until you start to internalize delight toward yourself. Starting a playful hobby like ice skating or dance might feel scary because it's new, not because it's a waste of time. Joy is healing. Fun, laughter, kindness, silliness even—they are all nourishing. And if we can't give them to ourselves, we're going to have a hell of a time trying to give them to our children!

Discovering the Joy Rampage!

I've woven a few helpful energy-shifting tools into this section, but I want to share one of my favorites. You can do it anywhere at any time. I like to call it a *Joy Rampage*. A Joy Rampage is like affirmations on steroids! Instead of just methodically spewing out affirmations, I speak to myself with whatever tone I need to hear in the moment. This is sometimes difficult to access in the moment. (That's why I call it a "rampage.") I allow the energy to build. I let affirmations flow until I have fully embraced whatever tone I need in order to fully feel the words. If I'm feeling sad, I speak to myself with love and compassion. If I'm feeling doubtful, I speak to myself with a powerful, convincing tone. We don't just need the words, we need the vibe! So speak to yourself like a best friend would speak to you. Or even better, speak to yourself like an intentional parent would speak to you.

I love using *I am* affirmations, but I find in the reparenting process that utilizing *you are* statements can be just as, if not more, effective. Doing this puts me in the position of the parent and allows me to speak directly to my inner child with whatever level of enthusiasm I may need. My Joy Rampage often starts out slow and unsure. If I'm sad, it can be really difficult to access compassion. And if I'm doubtful, it can be a challenge to access confidence. I just take it in small doses. And the more I speak, the more momentum I gain. So instead of just saying an affirmation like "I am powerful," I'll look at myself in the mirror and talk to my inner child. I'll say something like "Seriously, Destini? Come on, girl! You are so powerful. You can do anything. You are incredible. You are a creator. Look at all you've created. You can be afraid. But don't let it stop you!" (I'm honestly smiling as I'm writing this.) Talk about an energy boost! If that made you cringe, then maybe your inner child needs a different tone. Or maybe it's the exact tone you need and you just need to explore building the courage to try it. Either way, keep it personal to you. Try it by thinking about the biggest challenge you had today and then coach yourself through that challenge with "you are" statements. Remember to use language and a tone that truly resonates with what you need to hear. As you're coaching yourself through the moment, bring the energy. When you're affirming yourself, bring the energy. When you're scared and need some bravery, bring the energy. Let's go on a Joy Rampage!

If you're struggling to find a positive mindset, use the following journal prompt to shift your energy:

- What's the biggest challenge you had today? Coach yourself through that challenge with "you are" statements. Remember to use language and a tone that truly resonates with what you need to hear.

From Surviving To Thriving

(Creating Safety)

This chapter will change your life! No, seriously, it will. Now, I'm not going to give you some life-changing advice that doesn't end up changing anything but your mood for the day. Instead, I'm going to give you advice that will literally change your life by changing what is occurring in it. I'm talking about making some *external shifts.* Yes, we started with making internal shifts and making sure our awareness, acceptance, energy, and presence are all in alignment. But let's be honest: you want to actually *see* change. If you didn't care about that, you'd be meditating all day and not waking up and doing things to improve your life and well-being. The internal work helps us to take action that is rooted in wholeness, but we're not going to pretend it's just what happens on the inside that counts. Sure, we want to feel good, but we also want to live lives that don't suck. We want to have positive experiences. (There's nothing wrong with that!) We don't just want to convince ourselves that parenting is awesome, we actually want to enjoy it. But that does require action on our parts. So in this chapter we're going to talk about some actionable steps that can make parenting a whole lot easier and a whole lot more enjoyable.

Choosing to Take Control

There are certain experiences that can either support or undermine your parenting. Have you ever noticed that some days you can totally crush it? You have patience and compassion for your children and you are able to meet their needs and move through your day gracefully. And then there are the shit shows! Sometimes they can feel like the first day on a job. Have you ever stopped to wonder why that is? Have you ever gotten curious about what's different on those days? Sometimes it's internal. But even as your awareness, nonjudgment, energy, and presence shift, you will still find that your experiences have a significant impact on how you move through your day.

Fortunately, you have a choice. You can either continue to be at the whim of your conditioned experiences and just barely make it through your days or you can choose to master your environment by creating a space that supports your well-being. No, you cannot control everything that happens to you. And a large part of our resilience and perseverance comes from accepting the things we cannot change. However, there are so many elements of our day that we can positively impact. You are a creator, constantly shaping the world around you. You can create your life with more intention. And once you've committed to more awareness, nonjudgment, energy, and presence, you can make more conscious decisions about the world you create. This is a really kind thing to do for yourself and also for your child. When you feel confident, secure, and rooted in your space and your place in the world, you can more effectively offer that same environment to your child. Don't take for granted the power of your experiences. Take this chapter as an opportunity to see which areas of your well-being can be expanded. It's through this process that you can find balance. When you are clear on the areas of your life that need expansion, you can be intentional about filling your reservoir in those areas.

Before we get started, I want to make a note on survival mode parenting. Survival mode parenting is when your environmental,

mental, or emotional safety is extremely compromised. Environmentally, it could be something like a financial crisis. Mentally, it may look like a mental health crisis. Emotionally, it may be grieving the loss of a loved one. If you have ever been in a space where you're parenting from survival mode, you know how crippling it can be. Can you still make intentional decisions as a parent? Hell yeah! But you will struggle to thrive in your relationship with your child if all of your well-being is severely compromised. If you are in survival mode, I hope you find ways to prioritize yourself so that you can parent from an empowered space. You deserve to be safe and you deserve to give yourself grace through your process. I pray that abundant resources, tools, and support become clear in your path. And if you are in a dangerous situation, please put this book down and seek resources that can serve that immediate need. I'll be here when you get back. I promise!

You may not be in an extreme crisis or parenting in survival mode, but certain stimuli in our environments can still activate fight-or-flight responses in our brains, causing us to respond impulsively and erratically, rather than intentionally. Even the most subtle stimuli in your environment can significantly impact your well-being, creating internal experiences that are very similar to survival mode. While these stressors may not pose an immediate threat like abuse or lack of housing, over time they can cause a huge strain on your ability to show up as the parent you want to be. Some common stressors in physical environments might include financial troubles, uncomfortable living arrangements, inconsistent schedules or routines, unhealthy physical habits, an unstable support system, draining relationships, and unfulfilling activities. Let's look at them individually.

Finding Environmental Safety

Everything you do in your life is in some way connected to your need for safety. From the relationships you choose to how you spend your time, you are constantly meeting that need whether you realize it or not. So the most intentional way to shift your experiences is to look at the ways you are not currently providing yourself safety. The areas where you don't feel your safety needs are being met will need addressing and can significantly affect your parenting. If you don't have a strong sense of safety, you will struggle to provide it to your child. And they need that safety in order to develop healthy relationships, a positive self-image, and resilience.

Finances

We all have different financial baselines. What is considered "enough" money for your family might not be the same for my family. When it comes to establishing financial safety, you need to map out what your family needs to thrive. Knowing your financial baseline will help you recognize when your financial situation is the culprit for chaos in your environment. Sometimes that baseline can get thrown off due to a lack of savings or excess spending (or some random pandemic comes in and completely gut-punches your bank account). When you are not able to meet that financial baseline for your family, parenting can become a challenge.

We can't deny that there is a certain level of pressure that comes with parenting. It's one thing to have to provide for yourself, but when you're parenting you're taking care of other humans. And when you also have other mouths to feed, that's added pressure. If you are struggling to make ends meet, that can have a huge impact on your ability to parent consciously. It's really hard to be playful when you're feeling guilt about taking your kid out of soccer. It's really hard to not snap at your kids if you've gone unemployed for a fourth week in a row. (I can empathize with that!) If your finances are suffering, let me just say that it's normal to experience some chaos in your parenting.

When we don't feel secure, it's so much harder for us to regulate our emotional states. I have definitely had seasons in my life where my financial baseline was off. But I understood the connection between my environmental safety and my ability to parent in an aligned manner. This allowed me to have a bit of grace for myself on my journey back to financial security. It doesn't mean I let myself off the hook—I still had to empower myself and be intentional about shifting my financial situation—but in the meantime, as I did the repair I was conscious of the root cause of the chaos. I didn't create a shame story, and I was able to make changes from a place of empowerment rather than fear or unworthiness. You can take accountability and apologize to your children when you are a little less patient in these seasons. And then at night you can sit with yourself and say, "It's okay! I'm working through my financial situation. I will figure this out. It won't always be like this. I am learning the tools and getting the resources necessary for my family to thrive." And then you can move on and show up the next day with intention so you can more quickly get back to parenting in an environment that feels safe. Use this journal prompt as a way to become more connected with your financial safety:

- How do you feel when your finances are off? Does this impact your ability to parent with ease? (If you recognize that you are more frantic and irritable when your finances are off, this should not be ignored.)

Living Arrangements

Sometimes your environmental safety can be related to your living arrangements. Discomfort in your living space makes parenting from thrive mode a constant challenge. For example, if you've ever struggled to keep your space clean or organized, then you may know exactly what I'm talking about—shuffling through laundry piles to find the sock's mate; feeling anxious when you walk into a messy room; or being just a little on edge trying to play in a cluttered living room. All of these things make intentional parenting a bit harder. Even if your messiness doesn't cause you the same anxiety as it does me, I want you to think about how you feel when a space is clean. If the thought of a well-kept space brings you some ease, there's room to improve your well-being here. I know this was the case for me. When my home was disorganized, it wasn't because I was lazy, it was a result of my undiagnosed ADHD. I didn't know I had it until my late twenties, so I couldn't figure out why keeping a tidy home was an almost impossible feat. Most cleaning and organizing advice didn't work for me, so I constantly felt uneasy in my own home. I'd walk in the house and instantly feel stressed. This wasn't the best recipe for intentional parenting. I had to find the support and tools that would cater to my unique situation.

Another uncomfortable living arrangement I hear about often is living with in-laws, a parent, or a roommate. If you've ever been in this situation, you know just how difficult it can be to share space with other adults, especially if they don't agree with your parenting style. Not only can this impact your environmental safety, it can impact your children's, as well. It can also make it harder for you to parent with intention. Your intentions aren't the only ones that matter when you're in an uncomfortable living arrangement. Other people are impacted by your and your child's choices. I personally loved living with my parents when I first had my daughter. But was it easy? Absolutely not! Was I in thrive mode? I definitely was not. My parents and I bumped heads a lot because we had different opinions about how my daughter should be raised. Neither of us were right or wrong. We just had different views. And although the space was very loving, I can't deny that conflicting opinions can make parenting with ease and confidence much more difficult.

Maybe you don't feed your children sweets, but the grandparents do. Now you're dealing with a wild sugar baby that you didn't create who won't go to sleep until 1 a.m. Of course you're stressed out! Maybe every time you try to calmly talk through a situation with your child, your mother-in-law encourages you to just spank them! Or worse, she actually punishes them herself. I'm sure you can imagine how much easier it would be without those added opinions and influences.

4 From Surviving to Thriving

Or maybe you don't have as much space as you would like. Maybe you're all sharing a room. Of course that's going to make certain parenting tools a challenge. For a little while, we either lived in hotel rooms or stayed with a family member or friend. That meant the three of us were always on top of each other. And while it wasn't miserable, some parenting tools just weren't as easy to implement. How do you take a "space break" with no space? How do you do "special time" with one kid when you can't step away from the other one? These things aren't impossible, but the solutions can require much more mental and emotional effort.

So understand that intentional parenting with confidence may be more difficult in a physical environment that doesn't support it. But your living arrangements can change. Change is rarely quick or easy when it comes to your living arrangements. You are in your current living arrangement for a reason, so I would never diminish that by telling you to just change it right now. But you can still begin the process of moving toward something better suited for your well-being. If you are feeling stressed in your physical environment, consider what it would truly take to shift your living arrangements. There is a certain sense of security that comes with a clear plan, so take the time to look at what resources you'll need to implement that plan. What would you like your space to look and feel like? If you need to move, where would you like to live? How much money would you need to live there? What support do you need to begin this process? What is standing in the way of you making this change? For now, you can get creative about finding some temporary fixes that can shift the comfort level even just a bit. Maybe that's done by sectioning off the room so everyone has a designated area. Or maybe that's done by establishing small boundaries for yourself and your children.

In the meantime, please know that parenting intentionally in this type of situation, while more difficult, is still possible. You can still build a healthy, secure relationship with your child. It's also an opportunity for you to be aware and accepting of your environment so that you can show up with as much energy and presence as possible until things change. Remember, when you focus too much on things you can't immediately change, you can miss the areas where you can cultivate positive change right now. Even in an uncomfortable living situation, you have power over things like how you communicate, what you choose to give your energy to, and the amount of grace you give yourself during this time.

Schedules and Routines

Do you find it difficult to find consistency in your schedules or routines? Maybe some days you wake up at 6:00 a.m. and on other days you wake up at noon. If this sounds like you, ask yourself if this habit is affecting your ability to parent with intention. I'm not suggesting that you need to adhere to a strict schedule every day, but creating consistency in schedules and routines can be a powerful tool. If you know you have better parenting days when you wake up before your child, planning a consistent wake-up time for you might be of huge benefit to both of you, and thus a good intentional practice to implement. Adding a little more intention can give you and your children a chance to move through your day with more ease.

I thrive on freedom, so the idea of sticking to a strict daily schedule really annoys me. But now that I realize the positive impact that consistent routines can have on my day, I've found that adding a little bit of consistency can actually support my freedom. I love spontaneity and novelty, but there is something to be said about consistency that can keep us grounded. That's why I love *time anchors*. Time anchors are points in your day that have very little flexibility. Specific tasks like waking up, going to sleep, and cooking and eating meals are all tasks that can be anchored to specific times to ensure that you have the time to do the other things that give you joy! If I am committed to waking up between 5:00 a.m. and 6:15 a.m. every day, I give myself more room to play or meditate throughout the day. I'm more likely to lean into the things that naturally make parenting easier because I have the time to do them. Time anchors help me have the time for the things I truly love.

If you anchor dinner at 7:00 p.m., you can make more conscious decisions about other activities in your evening. Maybe that 5:00 p.m. play date at a friend's house isn't such a good idea, but maybe you can invite them to your home instead. Without time anchors, we can find ourselves saying "yes" to things in the moment that could cause friction later. Spontaneity is not something to run from in parenting; it's going to be chaotic and messy and free sometimes! But if you have certain things that anchor and ground you, you can experience a little more simplicity and a little less chaos. Anchors let us plan for our freedoms, delights, and play!

Here are my current time anchors and how they give me more flexibility and freedom:

- **Wake-up time for me: between 5:30 a.m. and 6:15 a.m.** (Waking up this early allows me to have time to myself.)

- **Wake-up time for the girls: between 6:30 a.m. and 7:00 a.m.** (Waking the girls at this time takes away the need to rush and makes our mornings easier.)

- **Dinner: between 6:00 p.m. and 6:30 p.m.** (Having dinner at this time allows us to move through our evening routine more slowly, which makes winding down much easier.)

- **Younger daughter's bedtime: between 8:45 p.m. and 9:30 p.m.** (Intentionally designating a bigger time block allows me to have one-on-one time with her before bed. That way I have more patience if she's overstimulated, needing extra attention, or anxious about bedtime. I am a lot less reactive when there's no sense of urgency.)

- **Older daughter's bedtime: between 9:30 p.m. and 10:15 p.m.** (The same flexibility holds true for my older daughter. A bigger time block leaves room for any bedtime challenges.)

- **My bedtime: between 10:30 p.m. and 11:15 p.m.**
(How quickly the girls get to bed determines how
much "me" time and sleep I'll get, but this anchor
ensures that I at least get a few minutes to myself and
at least seven hours of sleep.)

We do a whole bunch of other things throughout our day;
however, we schedule our other activities around our time anchors.
This is how I've created consistency in what used to be a pretty
hectic routine. Of course, this isn't something you'll figure out
overnight. It takes time to figure out the best time anchors for your
family. The girls used to have much earlier bedtimes, but there
was so much fuss that they ended up going to bed late anyway. My
younger daughter would get up twelve times and my older daughter
would move like a sloth, and I was the subpar ringmaster of the
entire circus. We wasted so much valuable time struggling through
the evening when we could have been connecting and easing into
bedtime. So I moved back the bedtimes, I let them play longer,
and it works for all of us. They still get eight to ten hours of sleep,
I still get to bed on time, and there is *a lot* less stress and anxiety.
Of course, we didn't get to this place overnight. It takes time to
create a system that is practical, so be patient with yourself and your
family. (To help you with this process, I have outlined some ways to
create an effective routine in a later chapter.)

Support Systems

Your support system is so important. We need people. It just is
what it is. We are communal creatures. Even the most introverted
of us need help and support in our parenting journeys. It's true
that parenting takes a village, but everyone's village won't be the
same. We all have a different need level when it comes to support,
but we can't do it all by ourselves. And whether you're married
or single, close to or far from relatives, or a part of a big or small
friend group, you don't have to do this alone! In fact, doing it
alone will make it harder for you and your child to thrive. Here's

the uncomfortable truth: you're not good at everything (we don't just download every single skill when we become parents), but you are the perfect parent for *your* child and there are things that other people can do to support you. There are spaces in this journey that you can have a greater impact in by simply asking for help.

I'm really good at teaching my daughter, but I'm not that great at teaching her during difficult life transitions. It was becoming a detriment to myself and my child to ignore this. I was beyond my capacity, and it wasn't fair to either of us. I wish I could say I recognized this earlier than I did, but the truth is my pride and my ego blinded me for a while and it was hurting her progress. When I realized this, I knew I had to lay down my pride and find support. So with a ton of deep breaths, I decided to put her in Montessori school. This was one of the hardest decisions I've ever made, but I knew I needed to expand my village, especially when I realized I had other resources available. Three years ago I would have felt so much shame about making this decision; after all, it was my idea to homeschool. But my desire for both of us to thrive outweighed my fear of looking like a failure. I had to lean on a new resource and be okay with the fact that I can't be everything for her. And thank goodness I recognized this! I'd be seriously stretched thin if I had continued to try to go it alone. Now she's thriving in school and I'm not holding on by a thread!

If you are having a difficult time feeling confident in your parenting, it may be time to take a look at your support system. I know this is easier said than done for some of us. Getting support can be a real challenge if you have limiting beliefs about asking for help. Maybe you think it's scary; maybe you think it makes you weak or incompetent; maybe you think your life will fall apart if you're not in control of every little thing. If any of this resonates with you, I want to tell you that you are not alone. I also want you to get curious about how these limiting beliefs are impacting your relationship with yourself and with your child. Is your lack of support causing your family harm? If so, how can you slowly ease into accepting support? Maybe you can start by affirming the fact that accepting support is okay! The next time you need help, consider responding to yourself the way that a supportive caregiver would respond to their child: "It's okay to need help. We all need help sometimes." The more you lean into that thought, the easier it will be to ask for help. And as you develop your support network and tap into it, you will find that you actually have more capacity to give back to yourself, your kids, and your community. And that giving will be from a place of intention and with a full cup, not from depletion and a false sense of obligation.

Sometimes you don't have the help you need because you genuinely don't know where to find it. If that's the case, get curious about sources of unconventional support! I really do wish we all had the support of our family and friends on our journeys. But that's simply not the case for many of us. Luckily, support comes in many different forms and sometimes we have to create our own communities. That might mean spending more time with people who don't look like you or putting yourself out there by joining online communities. That might mean being the kind of person who knocks on your neighbor's door to introduce yourself. That might mean actually participating in the PTA meeting instead of sitting in the back row, feeling annoyed, and waiting for it to end. For me, support looks like my online community, friends, family, my daughter's school, and of course, the "village chief," otherwise known as my therapist! Here are some journal prompts to help you along:

- What areas of your life could you use more support in?

- What would life look like if you had more help in these areas?

- What opportunities for connection and community are you currently avoiding? Why do you think you are avoiding them?

- What's one action you can take today to lean into
  community and support. (i.e., calling a friend, starting
  a conversation with another parent at pickup, or
  finding an online support group)?

Relationships

Speaking of people, let's talk about relationships. You cannot
separate the parent-child relationship from your relationships with
others. The energy we give to our friends, family, strangers, and
coworkers also impacts the energy that we are able to give to our
children. Take some time to look at your outside relationships and
ask yourself if those relationships are filling your cup. Are they
bringing you encouragement, joy, peace, and growth? Or are they
draining the life out of you? Sometimes you are going to be the
primary giver in relationships. And a slight imbalance isn't always a
sign that a relationship is unhealthy. We all move through different
seasons in our relationships, but it's important to ask yourself if
those relationships have had enough balance historically to cover
seasons of imbalance. If not, this is an opportunity to do some
auditing. Do you really have the capacity to keep watching your
sister's kids right now? How much is this business relationship
impacting your overall well-being? Do you have enough uplifting
relationships to handle your best friend's emotional needs right
now? Does the overall state of your core relationships make you
feel expansive or small? Make a list of the five people you interact
with most often and use the following journal prompts to explore
these questions:

- Do you interact with each person in ways that you'd
  like to interact with your children? (Don't consider
  the context. I'm not implying that you should be able
  to sip mimosas with your five-year-old; just consider
  the vibe.)
- Is there compassion, kindness, and empathy in these
  relationships?

- Are you comfortable setting and maintaining boundaries with each other?
- Do you both practice respectful communication?
- Are both of your needs being met?

Activities

How are you spending your days? Are you having a good time with this life thing? Maybe everything isn't going to be enjoyable, but are you doing the things you want to be doing most of the time? (You don't have to be like me and take a hard pass on stuff you absolutely don't want to do, but it's really freeing and totally an option!) Then again, maybe that's not what feels aligned for you. Is balancing joyful activities and your obligations possible? Do you have a hobby to balance out a soul-sucking job? Do you take time throughout your day to do things that put a smile on your face in between the things that are emotionally and mentally draining?

It's so easy to give every ounce of yourself away to the desires of others. Your boss needs this and your kids need that, but that's so disempowering. There are essential things you need in order to feel happy and alive! And the more you give yourself those things, the more magnetic you'll become to attract the safe environment we've been talking about in this chapter. I don't just mean this on a metaphysical level, either. When you fill yourself up first, you'll literally have more energy, clarity, and confidence to tackle your day. When you focus on things that matter to you, you will attract financial abundance, shifts in your environment, consistency, support, and healthy relationships. You'll attract them because you'll have the energy to put in the work to actually create them. That doesn't happen when you're following a life-draining to-do list! It comes from doing stuff you actually like to do. Here are some journal prompts to help you find activities that resonate with you:

- What activities do you do simply out of a sense of obligation?
- What activities bring you fulfillment and joy?
- If everything in life were free, you had all the time in the world, and you had absolutely no fear, what activities would you choose to do?

And whenever you are feeling insecure in your environment, you can return to these prompts to return to a place of intention:

- In general, do you feel safe?
- Do you feel comfortable with your financial situation?
- Are you comfortable with your living arrangements?
- Are you comfortable with your current schedule and routines?
- Do you feel safe with your support system?
- Are you comfortable with the quality of your relationships?
- Do you have enough enjoyment in your daily activities?

If you answer "no" to any of these questions, think about what you would like to see change and list three small things you can do in the coming weeks to make a shift in your environment. These things could include blocking that one person on social media (you know who), asking a family member for help, or setting up an automatic transfer to your savings account. Grounding, planning, and action are your best friends when you feel stuck in your environment. Return to your journal practice any time your environmental safety is negatively impacted during your parenting journey.

Finding Emotional and Mental Safety

When it comes to your sense of security, you also need to consider your emotional and mental safety. These two types of safety can oftentimes have an even greater impact on your parenting than safety in your physical environment.

Emotional Safety

Emotional safety is the degree to which you are able to acknowledge and accept your emotions. It's not about fixing or changing your emotions; we move through our emotions by giving them a safe space to exist, not by forcing them to go away. When we give ourselves emotional safety, we are intentional about holding space for whatever feelings come up. If you grew up in environments where some emotions were acceptable while others were not, it may be difficult for you to provide yourself with emotional safety. If you grew up hearing "Big girls don't cry," then you were not safe to acknowledge and accept sadness. In turn, this experience may make it difficult for you to deal with things like tantrums, whining, and meltdowns from your children. Likewise, when we don't effectively process our rage, we either internalize the emotions and direct them at ourselves, or we project them onto others.

In my childhood, my anger was not acceptable. And because I didn't have a safe space for my anger, I didn't really learn healthy ways to let it out. When you try to silence a child, they roar! And oh boy, did I roar, especially with the people closest to me. I can remember having so many angry fits in my childhood because I just genuinely did not know what to do with my emotions. The people around me weren't safe. But because I didn't have support in developing emotional regulation, I wasn't safe, either. When I became an adult, my anger just continued to cause more destruction. Except instead of being sent to my room, I was losing jobs, failing in relationships, and growing more distanced from

my family. Over time, I was able to gain peace in my interpersonal
relationships, but that rage was still there. Instead of directing it
at others, I began directing it toward myself. This made it difficult
to trust myself and for a long stretch of time I made decisions that
just expanded my rage. So much hurt was caused because I didn't
know how to manage my emotional state. So I began the work of
providing myself with emotional safety. I learned to witness my
anger without reactivity. And I started to practice this same kind
of awareness with all of my emotions. Rather than trying to force
them away or doing the opposite and allowing them to take over,
I got comfortable with them. I "invited them in" and got curious
about the messages they were trying to send me.

Mental Safety

It's a wonder any of us can even think for ourselves! Many of us
grew up being bombarded with the thoughts, opinions, and beliefs
of the adults around us. That's just how it works. As kids, we
adapted to our environments. Some of us were guided toward our
beliefs while others were pushed toward them. Maybe you grew
up in a home where you couldn't challenge the status quo. Maybe
your "survival" depended on you thinking and behaving like the
people around you. Simple expressions like a differing opinion or a
personal preference may have been taken as being disrespectful.

Growing up, I heard "You're so disrespectful" often as a child.
But looking back I know that a lot of that was simply just me having
my own thoughts and opinions. As I moved into womanhood,
I began to step away from the thoughts and beliefs that were
handed to me. I started paving the way for my own truth. I felt
like I was returning to my true self and writing a new story. But
in the beginning, I really struggled with trusting that story. Even
though the new narrative felt more aligned with who I believed I
was, I still lived in an environment that contradicted it. Though my
new thoughts and ideas were beginning to take shape, I continued
receiving messages all around me that made me question my new

story. Without that mental safety, my opinions, thoughts, desires, and beliefs could not take root and begin to impact my behavior and my life in a positive way.

We hear it all the time: "Think better thoughts" or "Be positive." But some of us don't really have the safest place to cultivate those thoughts. Quite frankly, after years of negative conditioning, my environment was probably the least productive place to form these "better" thoughts. So naturally that had a huge impact on my parenting. I was trying to convince myself to be an intentional parent when some of the people around me were advocating for the opposite! I was trying to affirm myself as the kind, compassionate woman I was becoming, but I was consistently hearing old messages about who I was in the past. In so many ways, I was trying to create new narratives around limiting beliefs and thoughts, but I was met with resistance in my environment. And it just made an already hard job—parenting—even harder.

So what are you to do? You've got all these ideas about parenting and breaking cycles, but does your current environment really support them? Do you genuinely have safety for your emotions, thoughts, and beliefs? Take a look at the following questions. They may give you a better idea!

Think again of the five people you talk to most regularly:

- Do they criticize the way you think?
- Do they make condescending comments about the things that are important to you?
- Do they dismiss your feelings?
- Do they struggle with just listening to your struggles, rather than trying to fix them?
- Do they let you get your thoughts out or do they often interrupt you?
- Do they see everything in black-and-white terms? (Everything is either all good or all bad.)

- Do they judge you for every little mistake you make?
- Are you hesitant to tell them good news?
- Do they constantly bring up past mistakes and fail to see any positive changes you've made?
- Are you hesitant to tell them difficult news because of how they've responded in the past?

I'm sure we can see at least some of these traits in all of our closest relationships. However, if these behaviors are dominating your circle I want you to consider that you may not have much emotional or mental safety right now.

Emotional safety means having a nonjudgmental space for your feelings, while mental safety means having a nonjudgmental space for your thoughts. These are actually really wonderful things to give yourself, especially if you didn't have them in your childhood. If you haven't heard it before, let me be the first to say it—your emotions are valid! Your beliefs and opinions do not have to align with those of the people around you. You're allowed to think differently than your family. You don't have to believe what your mother-in-law believes. You can have a vision for your family that looks completely different from your parents'. It's okay! You don't have to dishonor your truth anymore!

So let's do it. Let's prioritize your emotions, thoughts, and beliefs. Let's look again at that circle of five friends you identified earlier! Let's do some inventory of the conversations you're having with them. Could they be more productive? Is there room for growth there? Does this circle need to expand? Do you need a more supportive community for the thoughts you're trying to cultivate? And what about you? What about the internal conversations you're having with yourself? How much safety and nonjudgment are you giving your beliefs? Do you shoot yourself down the minute you come up with an idea? Are you constantly judging yourself for the mistakes you make?

Conditioning is a cycle that affects everyone in your circle. If you were conditioned to accept judgment of your thoughts and emotions, you will re-create this dynamic. You'll find friends and partners who judge you. And you'll continue to judge yourself. And, not surprisingly, judgment will also permeate your parent-child relationships. That is, unless you start providing yourself with more safety. So how do you do that? How do you give yourself more mental and emotional safety? You start by increasing your *conscious awareness*.

Conscious Awareness

I've found myself in more negative thought loops than I care to admit! But do you want to know the most challenging thought loop to break free from? It's the negative thought loop about the negative thought loop. That's a tough one! Have you ever been mad about being mad or felt guilty about feeling guilty? Most times, I don't need to change or ignore a thought, I just need to try my best not to add to it. When I add a negative judgment to the negative thought, I find it much more difficult to get back in control. This is why I choose conscious awareness by simply noticing my thoughts without judgment. I prefer to call it this, rather than meditation. Meditation means so many different things to different people. Many are taught that meditation is a clearing of the mind. But that description doesn't resonate with me at all. My mind isn't even clear when I'm asleep. And the more I try to force a clear mind, the more thoughts race into my head. Instead, I choose to practice intentional, conscious awareness. I just sit quietly and gently focus on my thoughts. Maybe I'll light a candle, maybe I won't. Sometimes I'll do it on a yoga mat and sometimes I do it while I'm folding clothes. Sometimes I take really deep breaths. Sometimes I breathe naturally. What matters most for me is the awareness. It's just a gentle noticing of my thoughts. I welcome them, I let them come through, and most importantly I don't try to change them. It's like watching a movie. You don't add to the story line. You don't change the characters or the plot. You just watch it and then you move on. This is how I meditate and I can do it anywhere and at any time of the day. It's the easiest way for me to create a safe space to process my thoughts.

The same is true for emotions. When a feeling comes up, just try to recognize it. This can help create space between the feelings and the resulting actions. Don't wait until you're screaming at the top of your lungs to acknowledge your anger. Don't wait until you're completely spiraling to acknowledge your sadness. The sooner you can recognize the feeling, the easier it will become to move through it. (All throughout my day I will acknowledge my emotions by using phrases like "I am feeling sad" or "I am feeling frustrated.") Just like with your thoughts, all you have to do is watch the movie. You don't have to try to force the feelings to change. Your emotions come up for a reason. At no point is your rage, fear, guilt, or sadness unacceptable. While every resulting behavior may not be acceptable, the emotions themselves are acceptable. And honestly, the better you become at integrating your emotions, the easier it will be to behave in ways that are in alignment with your values.

Imagine this same practice with a child. When we can recognize our anger before it takes over, it becomes much easier to choose responses that aren't forceful, aggressive, or punitive. But when we fail to notice the anger brewing, it can become damn near impossible not to yell, spank, or punish. This is why conscious awareness is so powerful. It can help us pause so that our thoughts and emotions don't get in the driver's seat for our behaviors.

Mood Tracking

Another effective way to give yourself emotional safety is to track your moods. Finding a few times in your day to check in with your emotions will help you become more aware of them. In the beginning of my intentional healing journey, this was a really helpful way to notice all of the emotions I was unconsciously experiencing throughout the day. Though I was not consciously aware of my emotional experience, the feelings were still very much impacting my behavior. So I set three alarms that went off at various points of my day. The notification on my phone simply said "How are you feeling?" This was an effective cue to stop and reflect on the feeling. I'd just stop, jot down the emotion, take a deep breath, and continue with my day. Being able to look back at my emotions was a really helpful way to recognize patterns and dominant emotions! (Back then I did this in a notepad, but there are so many mood tracking apps now that let you do this directly on your phone.)

Journaling

Journaling is a great way to process things. Using prompts like the ones in this book can help you get more comfortable with your thoughts and beliefs. With a simple Google search, you can find writing prompts on just about any topic. There are also some really great books with daily journal prompts. It's pretty cool to see how answering random questions can teach you so much about yourself and the way you think.

Another great journaling practice is *reflective journaling*. The goal with reflective journaling is to hash out your thoughts about a specific event. You can do this at the end of each day like I do or you can journal about a past experience. You can do this for both pleasant and unpleasant experiences. We talked about ruminating before and how harmful it can be. Writing can help you process your experiences rather than getting caught in unhealthy thought loops. Reflective journaling quite literally slows your thoughts down and allows you to release built-up emotions and see things through a more rational lens.

Probably my favorite type of journaling is *stream-of-consciousness journaling*. If you really want to know what's going on inside your head, try it. All you do is write whatever comes to mind in the moment. That's it! The only rules I stick to are having a designated page count or a time limit. I'll either do ten minutes or three pages, whichever I have time for, but other than that there aren't any rules.

I don't use prompts or guides and I don't care about grammar, punctuation, or handwriting. Oftentimes my handwriting isn't even legible. The thoughts are disorganized and some of it probably makes very little sense, but the whole point is to not overthink it and to just let the thoughts flow. At first it feels kind of strange to write whatever pops into your head. But sometimes it can be really profound and enlightening. Other times it will be utter nonsense. (Once I wrote, "the poppyseed peacocks are invading Toyland." I don't think it gets much more ridiculous than that!) But whatever comes to my mind, I write it down and this practice often leaves me feeling more calm, present, aware, and creative. It's like exiting out of all the windows and apps that are slowing your computer down. Without all of those thoughts running through your conscious and subconscious minds, you're able to think much more clearly. And that can have benefits in just about every area of your life!

Therapy

This last option takes a little more effort than the other two, but with more effort often comes greater effectiveness. The right therapist can provide you with a safe space to get your emotions out. There are so many types of therapy, but the options that have been most helpful for me are CBT (cognitive behavioral therapy), MBCT (mindfulness-based cognitive therapy), and for seasons when I was experiencing my feelings very intensely, DBT (dialectical behavior therapy). I have also done specific modalities like EMDR (eye movement desensitization and reprocessing) and EFT (emotional focused therapy) to better process my trauma. Though some worked better than others, all of these therapies were effective in helping me recognize and process my emotions. I know there is still a stigma attached to therapy, but if you still feel a bit of apprehension toward it, I'd like to invite you to see therapy as another tool in your tool belt. That's it. When we need to learn about a topic, books are a great tool. When we want to learn a new skill, practice is a great tool. And, when we want to learn about our thoughts and emotions, therapy is a great tool! Therapy is so much more accessible than it was in the past. So if you are having a hard time acknowledging your emotions before they take over your behaviors, I would highly recommend finding a therapist who you feel comfortable with.

I have a lot of sayings in my house. One that I say often is "Safety is non-negotiable." It is my hope that on your journey you begin to take your own safety seriously. Ease and flow are possible, but only if we are being intentional about creating a safe space that supports our well-being.

5

The Moat That Guards the Castle
(Setting Boundaries)

As we begin to shift our level of safety, there are going to be what I like to call "security breaches." Some people will inevitably get in the way of our safety. That's how life works. We can't control every little thing that happens to us. However, we can respond by establishing boundaries. Our boundaries are the firewalls that we set between ourselves and other people. Think of them as "the moat that guards the castle."

Defining Boundaries

Boundaries are the rules and limits that we create to communicate how people can access our time, energy, resources, and physical space. As we begin to set up our lives in ways that are conducive to our personal growth, we need to put some space between our well-being and other people's behaviors. When someone or something tries to disrupt our safety, it can have a major impact on our ability to parent from an intentional space. So it's our responsibility to make sure that doesn't happen. Many of us grew up in homes where we weren't allowed to set boundaries. Maybe you had to hug family members even when you felt uncomfortable doing so. Maybe your parents regularly invaded your privacy or used insulting language with you. As a result, you might have a difficult time setting and keeping boundaries. But it is an act of self-love and self-compassion to keep your time, resources, and space safe. As you begin to identify the things that make you feel safe, you get to give yourself protection. You get to analyze and assess the things that either add to or take away from your ability to create the life you desire. You get to set limits when anything infringes upon your peace. Why? Because your peace and well-being are nonnegotiable when it comes to being an intentional parent. I'm not suggesting you become rigid and inflexible, I'm simply suggesting that using a little more intention with how you let others treat you might impact your well-being in ways that will benefit not only you but your entire family. If you're making it through daily life with very few established boundaries, imagine how much of a phenomenal parent you will be when you start limiting the access that others have to your energy.

Beginning with "No"

Can you survive parenting with only fragile boundaries? Yes. But our goal as empowered parents is to thrive! And in order to thrive, you have to be willing to say "no" to the things that infringe on your environmental, mental, and emotional safety. A mother is able to say "no" when someone tries to feed her child peanuts when the child has a nut allergy. A father would fervently resist if a stranger tried to pick his child up. Now that you're an adult, it's your job to keep yourself safe. You're the parent now. Sure, we parent our kids, but let's be honest, we're still raising ourselves every single day. And much of the reparenting process is about protecting ourselves from things that put us in danger. Of course, the types of threats we face as adults are a bit different now, but that doesn't mean we don't move through our days with possible security breaches. We all do and they absolutely affect how we show up as parents. So when someone or something comes to disrupt your peace, I would like you to visualize yourself as the devoted parent rushing in to save the day. Step in with love and intention and defend your safety. If you know you need a peaceful environment in order to feel emotionally safe, then you need some boundaries. Maybe you can't talk to your cousin on the way home because she's got too much drama in the moment, so you only talk to her once your kids go to bed and you're done interacting with them for the day. If you've created a schedule that works for you and your family, you need to establish some boundaries to make sure you can maintain it. Maybe your mother-in-law can't visit during the week. Maybe now you still can't talk to that cousin after the kids go to bed because you have to wake up early to keep your routine. And maybe you need to set limits on the kinds of conversations you're willing to have with her. Not only is this important for you, but it's also important for your children's well-being. Modeling healthy boundaries and teaching them how to set and maintain their own will help your children to develop a secure sense of self. It will also help them navigate interpersonal relationships and respect other people's boundaries. Everything is connected to what we are and also what we are not willing to put up with. Our eating habits? They're based on our boundaries. The quality of our relationships and friendships? It's based on our boundaries. Our career, social, and spiritual lives? They're defined by our boundaries. Basically our quality of life has a whole lot to do with how intentional we are about knowing, articulating, and honoring our boundaries.

The Five-Step Boundary-Setting Process

So what does the process of setting boundaries actually look like? Well, boundaries are complex because humans are complex. But that doesn't mean we can't have a framework. The following steps are how I practice setting boundaries. The degree to which you need to home in on each step will vary based on the situation and the person you are setting your limits with. However, I've found that the more I practice this process the better I get at it, regardless of the specifics of the situation. It's like building a muscle. It's a complicated process, but the more you work at it, the better you get at understanding what you need in order to see positive results. So let's do it. Here is my four-step boundary-setting process!

Step 1: Clarify Your Needs

The first step to defining your boundaries is understanding who you are within your world and paying close attention to your needs. In the previous chapter, you learned about your environmental, emotional, and mental needs. And the better you become at understanding what it is you need in your environment, the better you will become at establishing boundaries with the people around you. The better you are at knowing what you need emotionally and mentally, the better you will become at setting boundaries that will serve your thoughts and feelings. If you're struggling to identify these things, it might be helpful to return to the journal prompts from the previous chapter. Oftentimes as parents we put ourselves on the back burner. We are committed to improving the lives of our children and are constantly moving mountains for them. We are often very familiar with their needs, but not always with our own. *You* deserve to have your needs met. And *you* deserve to feel safe in your environment, so pause, take three deep breaths, and repeat the following affirmations to yourself:

I deserve to have my needs met.

I deserve to feel safe in my environment.

And then ask yourself:

What do I need in this moment?

Here are some responses that may come to mind as you ask yourself this very important question:

- I need more rest.
- I need an outlet to express my emotions.

- I need more financial stability.

- I need more fun and fulfillment.

- I need more quiet time to myself.

- I need more exercise and movement.

- I need time to process my grief.

- I need a cleaner space.

The question you just asked yourself is a really important one. And I hope you learn to check in with your needs more often. Meeting your own physical, emotional, and mental needs is one of the greatest pathways to intentional parenting. And the boundary decisions you'll make will be based on the needs you identify.

Step 2: Define Your Boundaries

As you work to define your boundaries, think of yourself as a researcher and your life as an experiment. Your days are filled with data—from the moment you wake up to the moment you close your eyes to go to sleep, you are receiving information. The better you become at making observations throughout your day, the easier it will become to define your personal needs and boundaries. You can start the process by making observations about how you feel after you perform certain activities or when you spend time with certain people. If your yoga practice makes you feel grounded but Instagram makes you feel anxious, that's a clear sign that you need more yoga and less Instagram! If you feel joyful around some friends but depleted around others, that's a sign that you need to create some boundaries to protect your most empowering relationships and also create boundaries that enhance the quality of the not-so-empowering ones. When you walk through life with a more conscious awareness of what's happening around you, you are more readily able to create the life that you desire. And when you are filled up, excited, and intensely fulfilled, that energy and intention will spill over into your parenting. You will move through your days more consciously. You won't just do things—you will do things with awareness! This kind of empowered shift supersedes any parenting tool or technique. Why? Because the more aware you become of your own needs and the boundaries required to fulfill those needs, the easier it will be to intuitively know what your family needs at any given moment.

So as you begin to sift through your day and uncover the boundaries you need to establish in order to thrive, you'll need to understand what you need to accomplish in order to ensure that those needs are met. Understanding what gets in the way of meeting your needs is just as important as understanding the needs themselves. This is where you begin to create boundaries. Once you have an understanding of what is holding you back, you can explore what it will take to change the situation. To start the process, think about each of the following areas of your life:

- Environment
- Physical health
- Relationships
- Career/work
- Spiritual life
- Finances
- Passions

Next, identify a disturbance in each of these areas by asking yourself what is standing in the way of you getting your needs met. Your responses should be empowering and self-focused. For example, "I need my mom to stop saying mean things about my body" is not an empowered, you-centered statement; however, "I need to limit the conversations I have with my mom" is. And while the boundaries you set will likely involve your mom, the need you identify should be focused solely on you and what you can control. Once you've identified the need, you can create the boundary for each of the seven aforementioned areas by defining an action you can take to stop allowing these people or things to stand in your way. You can come back to this process as often as you like, but start small; it's much easier to stick to your boundaries if you can focus on them one at a time. Once you get into a new rhythm and feel the impact of the boundary, you can confidently move on to addressing the next disturbance! It's also important to remember that the severity of your boundary will depend on the degree to which the disturbance is affecting your life. For instance, if you need more sleep but you are staying up all night answering emails from clients, you need to create a boundary. You might begin by cutting your emails off an hour earlier so that you can get a bit more rest. For your finances, you might have a friend who keeps asking to borrow money and it's beginning to affect your financial situation and your friendship. While you probably won't need to cut that person off completely, this may be an opportunity to limit the financial resources you are willing to share with them. On a more severe level, you may have someone in your life who is constantly hurting you mentally, physically, or emotionally, so you may need to set a stricter boundary and only interact with them when absolutely necessary or not at all. The intensity of the boundary will depend on how intensely the person or thing is impacting your well-being. No one can define these boundaries for you. They have to be rooted in what feels right for you. That is why a deep level of self-awareness in this process is important. If you don't understand what you need in order to feel safe, you'll have a difficult time setting boundaries. However, when you are in harmony with your safety needs, setting boundaries will become significantly easier.

Step 5: Communicate Your Needs

One of the most important things you can do when establishing a boundary is communicating your needs. As you begin taking responsibility for your time, energy, and resources by setting boundaries, it may come as a shock to some people. And understandably so. Change is difficult for many people. But clear communication lets people know exactly what to expect and what you will and will not tolerate in your relationships going forward. With that said, communication isn't everyone's strong suit. And communication often needs to be tailored to individuals and the situations. Here are some principles for making communication a bit more effective as you begin setting boundaries.

Use Communication That Is "You-Centered"

When you are aware of your needs, you can articulate them with sentences that begin with you-focused phrases like "I need," "I would like," and "I prefer." Here's why this is important: in order to effectively articulate your boundaries, you need to focus your communication more on your needs and less on the other person's behaviors. Focusing on the other person's behaviors will likely make them feel inclined to defend said behaviors. I wish defensiveness weren't such a common response to criticism, but it often is. So it's okay to be tactful and keep in mind that the main goal isn't to be right, condemn, or argue, it's to set a boundary. It's also important to be aware of your conditioned responses. When people become defensive in conversations, do you revert to a fight, flight, freeze, or fawn response? If so, this can set the conversation off course. If you are a fighter, you may respond more aggressively and begin criticizing the other person more harshly, which will move you further and further away from your actual need. This can often lead to a more severe boundary being put into place unnecessarily: "Fine, Dad. Since you're so selfish we don't have to talk at all!" If flight is your go-to response, you'll potentially run from the subject, either diminishing your needs or abandoning the boundary altogether. This, of course, means that you will continue the relationship in a way that doesn't allow you to get your needs met: "You know what, I can figure this out later. *So what was your day like?*" If you are a freezer, you may completely shut down and discontinue the conversation: "I have to go. Bye." In some cases you may need time to reflect and return to a conversation; however, if you never return to the conversation with clear communication, your needs will be left unmet. If you are a fawner, you may go into "people-pleasing" mode and start agreeing with the other person or implying that the boundary wasn't all that important to you in the first place: "Now that I think about it, you're right, Mom. You have done a lot for me and it's silly of me not to want to help you out right now."

In one way or another, defensiveness will likely get in the way of boundary setting. That's why it's best to steer clear of judging the other person's behavior as good or bad or right or wrong. Rather, you can acknowledge what is helpful or harmful for your well-being. That way, you can have a judgment-free conversation about what you need to feel most comfortable in the relationship and make requests based on those needs. For example, if you are more focused on the other person's behavior, you might say, "You've been feeding my kids junk food. Junk food is bad for them and that has to stop if you're going to keep them." The other person would likely feel attacked, even if they care very deeply about you and your children. Conversely, if you said, "I would prefer them not to eat junk food." You don't need to convince the other person that junk food is bad. You just need to express to them that it's a boundary that you're setting for you and your family and you're requesting that it be respected.

Use Communication That Is Compassionate

In these conversations, it's important to remember that we are talking to other humans who also have feelings and deeply rooted beliefs. It would be foolish of us not to consider those feelings in the ways we communicate. Don't get me wrong. There will be times when people just don't deserve your presence. But in many instances it can be helpful to first give people an opportunity to repair their behaviors. We can communicate our expectations in a compassionate way before we burn bridges. So when you approach a boundary-setting conversation, ask yourself if you want to be heard or understood. If you just want to be heard, then you can go full force with the blame, shame, and judgment. But if you really want your needs to be met and also still respect the other person in the conversation, you should go in with compassion. If you desire to set a boundary and still keep the relationship intact, you should lead with empathy. Establishing boundaries can be scary, especially if your relationships don't have many. And if you don't approach your communication with intention, setting a boundary can tear down a relationship; however, when we are conscious of how we set boundaries, they can actually enhance the quality of our relationships.

How do we use compassion in our communication? There are three things that can make communication more compassionate: *calmness, clarity,* and *courteousness. Calmness* means we express our boundaries when we are emotionally regulated. When you feel at ease and can process your needs and feelings gracefully, you can set a boundary compassionately. If you are enraged, however, you will not be able to express yourself effectively. Remember: we want to be understood, not just heard. It's like what I say to my kids sometimes: don't let your message get caught in your mess! If you have a need, then you have a message that you need to convey. But if you express that message in the heat of emotion, you're more likely to convey it poorly and then the need will go unmet and the relationship will be negatively affected. Again, if your goal is to set the boundary and keep the relationship intact, you have to approach the conversation when you're in a state of calm. Let's go back to our junk food example. If you walk into your mother-in-law's house and see your kids stuffing their faces with candy, ask yourself, "How is this making me feel?" If you are slightly upset, maybe you can take a deep breath and address it in the moment. But if you are furious, you won't be able to address your boundary with compassion. Grab your little ones, say "thank you," and roll out! Come back to the conversation when you've returned to calm.

Now let's talk about *clarity.* Being able to clearly articulate your expectations is crucial. Many of us can express what we *don't* want. Are you able to express what you *do* want? People won't know how to treat you if you can't tell them how you want to be treated! How can someone meet an expectation when they're not completely sure of the expectation? They can't! So back to the junk food example, if your communication is simply you-focused, you may state that you would prefer them to not eat junk food. But when we consider clear expectations, you might take that a step further and say something like "I would prefer them not to eat junk food. When they're craving something sweet, I give them fruit." Now the expectation is clear—give my kid fruit instead of junk food!

Once you've communicated calmly and clearly, you can add a little *courteousness*. One of my favorite ways to do this is by requesting rather than demanding. Yes, both parties have to be willing to agree to a boundary in order for it to stick. But you don't have to force compliance. Instead, leave space for the other person to choose whether or not they can commit to the boundary. Again, this often puts the other person's defenses down. The conversation could look something like this: "I would prefer them not to eat junk food. When they're craving something sweet, I give them fruit. Do you think you could honor that and give them fruit, instead?" There's a clear request here: "Can you do this?" is much more courteous than "Don't do this." If you're feeling a little bothered by the idea of being courteous to someone who is doing something you don't like, I'd like to remind you of your original goal in setting the boundary, which is getting your needs met. If you didn't want this person in your life, you'd just cut them off, but at least a part of you wants this boundary-setting process to work, right? So you have to be courteous and respectful in your communication. If that's too difficult in the moment, wait until you can access that calm state we talked about earlier. It's okay to take a pause on the communication until you can offer them that courteousness and compassion.

Use Communication That Is Confident

Stop explaining your needs! I'm not suggesting you shouldn't divulge why you're setting a boundary. Explaining the boundary is just fair, effective communication. There's nothing wrong with telling your grandmother why you won't be coming to Sunday dinner for the next two months. However, when you start to explain the need itself, you can move into pretty tricky territory. For example, if you're not going to Sunday dinner because you are starting a yoga class to help you with your anxiety, you don't have to explain why that's important to you. You don't owe anyone an explanation of your needs. They are valid, whether someone else agrees with them or not. If you need more rest, time to yourself, kind communication, or positive friendships, those are valid needs. And if you struggle with setting boundaries, you may likely explain yourself right out of the boundary if you feel compelled to explain the reasoning. Your explanation is an easy setup for the other person's criticism of your needs. And you may end up conceding and ignoring the changes you're trying to make for yourself and your family. So don't explain yourself too much. Just make the request.

Step 4: Communicate Your Boundaries

Up until this point in the boundary-setting process, we have only discussed how to make requests about your needs. These requests are more like rules for the relationship, but they aren't actually boundaries. A rule is something that limits someone else's behavior. But the thing about a rule is that it places your well-being into someone else's hands. In the junk food example, making a request for your mother-in-law to give your kids fruit is a great first step, but it's not a boundary. It's just a rule, and she has a lot of power over whether or not your kids get junk food in the future. Sometimes people respect our rules. However, if that rule is not respected, it's time to set a boundary. Unlike a rule, a boundary is something that limits your behavior. Where a rule makes a request of the other person's future behavior ("can you"; "will you"), a boundary makes a statement about your future behavior ("I'm not willing to"; "I won't allow you to"). The latter is much more empowering. That way, whether the other person's behavior changes or not, your need is still getting met. So if your mother-in-law doesn't respect the rule, then you can proceed with the following boundary: "I told you I prefer them not to eat junk food. I asked you to give them fruit when they're craving something sweet. That request has not been respected. I love that they get to spend time with you, but if this happens again, they won't be able to visit without me."

Step 5: Commit to the Process

The last step in the boundary-setting process is committing to the process. Boundaries don't always catch on right away. Some relationships have deep conditioning. If you've been interacting with someone a certain way for years, you can't expect that to just change overnight. You'll probably both need an adjustment phase before it all begins to stick. But as I stated before, both parties have to commit to the goal. Sometimes the person receiving the boundary isn't able to commit. The other person may refuse your request or consistently neglect your boundary. Whether this neglect is intentional or just accidental, it's still your job to uphold the boundary. That is where your level of commitment comes into play. How committed are you to your safety? How committed are you to your well-being? When your cousin calls on your way home from work, do you ignore her and text her to remind her of the boundary? Or do you answer the phone and dishonor the boundary you've set? If you're new to boundary setting, your commitment level may be low. So I'd like to offer some very simple ways to increase your level of commitment:

1. **Get support.** Have people in your corner who will honor and respect you enough to tell you when you're not staying committed to your boundaries. Just like a gym buddy can make exercise a little bit easier, a boundary buddy can remind you to respect yourself. I love that my friends check me whenever I'm not staying committed to my boundaries; however, I know that not every relationship is like that. If your friendships aren't currently a space for accountability, that may be a great opportunity to give your friends permission to hold you accountable. In the beginning, some

of my friends wouldn't tell me when I was slacking. I have a really big personality and I'm not the most inviting when it comes to unsolicited opinions, so I had to give my friends permission to tell me about myself! I know they have good intentions, so if I'm ever not as committed as I need to be, they know they can come to me and keep it real. But that's only because I made that request. If you can't rely on your friends for that level of honesty or if you don't have much of a friend group, consider other people in your life who can support you in your boundary commitments. This may be a partner, a family member, or one of my favorite supporters: a good therapist!

2. **Practice often.** Take small baby steps toward setting boundaries. Practice using you-focused, clear, compassionate language as often as you can. You'll be surprised at how many opportunities there are to empower yourself throughout your day.

"Excuse me, waiter… " (Calm)

"… I would like my food a bit hotter… " (You-focused)

"… I'd like the cook to warm it up… " (Clear)

"… Can you take it back for me please?" (Courteous)

This isn't about being picky or particular. Remember: you deserve to have your needs met. Relationships are allowed to be equitable. If you're paying for something, it's okay to make a clear, courteous request. The same goes for any other give-and-take situation. At work? Make requests. In your friendships? Make requests. Your well-being matters. You can't spend all day responding to requests. You get to make some requests, too! Go for it. The better you get at the small boundary requests, the easier it will be to commit to the bigger ones.

3. Know when to fold 'em. What happens when someone doesn't respect your me-focused, compassionate boundary request? Well, honestly, that's up to you. You have to know your capacity and your limits. You might end a relationship and situation for completely different reasons than I would. The key is to trust your own intuition. As we grow in our self-awareness, we become much more in tune with our inner voices. Listen to that voice. And, when it tells you you're done with a relationship, be okay with that. Ultimately, you have to keep yourself safe. If something or someone is infringing on your well-being in a way that you cannot accept, you have to make a decision for yourself. Pray about it. Meditate on it. Sleep on it. Do whatever you have to do so that you can make the most clear, self-aligned choice possible. And if you choose to take that route, commit to it. That means that you don't let someone return to their previous level of access until they have clearly exhibited changed behavior *and* you are comfortable and ready for them to do so. Remember: you can forgive someone without giving them an opportunity to disrespect your boundaries again.

As you work to set your boundaries and create safety for yourself, I would like to share these affirmations that will help you in journey:

- I deserve to feel safe.
- I can keep myself safe.
- I deserve to have my needs met.
- Communicating my boundaries is easy.
- When I speak, I do so with clarity and compassion.
- My relationships improve based on my ability to set boundaries.
- My boundaries increase my well-being.

- I am safer with boundaries.
- I show myself love by setting boundaries.
- The more I honor my boundaries, the more confident I will become.
- I am attracting people who can accept, honor, and respect my boundaries.
- I deserve to be happy.
- My relationships are equitable. I receive just as much as I give.
- Every day I am learning more about who I am and what I need.

6

How to Not Lose Your Shit
(Understanding Your Triggers)

You're running late for a birthday party. You got up early but that doesn't matter because you have kids. You have to get everyone ready, all while managing the random obstacles associated with getting out of the house. You're just about ready to leave when you look at your little one and ask if she wants to wear the blue shoes or the black shoes. You give her options because you read somewhere that giving options works well in these kinds of situations. She smiles at you and says, "Mommy, I want my pink shoes."

Normally this would be just fine, except you threw away those god-awful pink shoes because a buckle was broken. You take a deep breath and prepare yourself for the coming tantrum. "Baby, our pink shoes went bye-bye. How about the black or blue shoes?" Within seconds, a tornado of emotion floods your daughter and she is in a full-blown spiral. Almost unconsciously, you look at her and yell, "I'm sorry, but we have to go. I don't have time for this. Pick now or I'm picking for you."

What happened here? Is your daughter overly sensitive? And how inconsiderate of her! Doesn't she know you're late? You used to always be on time, but now you're known for being late. I mean, it's a pair of shoes, right? And she's just going to wind up taking them off and throwing them anyway. Plus, she just told you last week that she hated her pink shoes. That's why you weren't hesitant about throwing them away.

Or maybe you're just a horrible parent! Damn! That's all it took for you to completely lose it? Why don't you care? She's crying and you're her parent. You're supposed to be warm and loving. Shouldn't you feel at least a little empathetic? No matter how hard you try, you can't seem to manage the tantrums.

It all sounds crazy, right? And whether or not you've experienced this situation or something similar, it's not unusual for a parent to feel this way. But if we're being realistic, your child's inflexibility isn't the reason for your reactivity. And your parenting abilities probably aren't to blame either. Oftentimes, we cling to the least likely explanations for our high-stress moments with our children. But the truth is, when we are reactive, the real reason probably has something to do with our triggers. When we are triggered, we are experiencing an unconscious mental and physical reaction to a stimulus in the environment. That means your brain and body respond when you are triggered before you do. There is both responsibility and grace within that truth. You are responsible for how you respond to your child, and at the same time when you are initially triggered it is a deeply conditioned physiological response that isn't completely in your conscious control. The good news is you can start to notice those triggering moments so you don't react so unconsciously. Furthermore, with practice, you can begin to rewire your physiology and train your brain toward less reactivity. But before all of that, you first have to get familiar with your triggers.

Recognizing Your Triggers

I'd be lying if I said my children don't get on my last nerve! They, like all humans, can evoke frustration, fear, shame, and most commonly for myself, anger. In fact, I think our children can sometimes be the most triggering people in our lives. For most of us, parenthood is the first time someone actually needs you. Your partner would survive without you. So would your boss, friends, and coworkers. But your kids quite literally need you. It's the relationship we can't run from. You can't break up with your children. (And I'm assuming you don't want to because you're reading this book.)

Maybe your temples start to throb when you hear "Mommy" for the tenth time in a row. Or maybe your heart starts to race when you realize your teenager didn't do the dishes again. My chest literally tightens when my daughter cries loudly in the middle of the night. Yup, that's right. I cannot stand a toddler crying sometimes! It doesn't mean I can't show up with love and empathy. It just means it overwhelms me—tremendously! This is one of my triggers. But I can say, "Hey, body, you're doing that chest tightening thing. Let's calm that down before I respond."

Very early on in the parenting experience I realized there was nowhere to run. The closer I got to my daughters and the more time we spent together, the more they would trigger me. And guess what? I'm totally comfortable saying that now. Admitting that my children can annoy the hell out of me has actually become one of my most useful tools as a parent. I know that most parenting narratives have fooled many of us into believing that we're supposed to enjoy parenting 24/7, but that is a highly toxic archetype that no one can live up to. You know you can't stand your kids sometimes, and if you can't admit it you won't learn how to effectively move through your triggers. The more you ignore your triggers, the louder they will roar.

Sure, I can calm myself, but the physical response is out of my control. In fact, I like to think of my triggers like my children: they live here. Most times I'm able to handle them; other times they handle me. Either way, they can teach me a great deal if I'm open.

You may not have heard this before but you are allowed to be angry with your child. It's normal to not like the parenting process sometimes. In fact, it's your ability to admit your triggers that gives you power over them. Plus, the more you are able to accept your own feelings, the easier it will be to accept your children's.

Common Triggers

In this section, I list some of the most common triggers I notice in my clients, along with some journaling prompts. See which triggers resonate with you and then use the journal prompts to explore them more deeply. In each journaling section, I ask how you feel when you are triggered. I think it's helpful to stick to the basic emotions—sadness, happiness, fear, anger, surprise, and disgust—when describing our feelings. But try not to limit your language too much. If "I feel pissed" is more true for you than "I feel mad," express that authentically. The goal is to notice how you feel when you're triggered. It's also helpful to describe the actual emotion ("I feel frustrated") rather than an interpretation or judgment ("I feel like she's being inflexible"). Here is a list of common emotions that come up when we're triggered:

- Angry
- Anxious
- Apathetic
- Ashamed
- Confused
- Critical
- Depressed
- Discouraged
- Embarrassed
- Frustrated
- Furious

- Guilty
- Helpless
- Inferior
- Insecure
- Insignificant
- Irritated
- Jealous
- Lonely
- Rejected
- Weak

In the prompts, I also ask how you respond to your triggers. When answering, think of the following responses:

- Fight (punishing, yelling, blaming, shaming, spanking)
- Flight (physically walking away)
- Freeze (shutting down, dissociating)
- Fawn (appeasing, ignoring your own needs)

As you do this exercise, please be graceful with yourself. Looking at your reactivity can be difficult, but it's also a really brave thing to do. You're doing a really good thing for yourself and your family by taking this step.

Crying

Crying can be a trigger for many parents. Some of you Level-10 Zen Master parents are unfazed by the screeching, while the rest of us may struggle with the crying. And this can continue as our children get older. Sometimes it's the noise itself that can be overwhelming for parents. For others, it may bring up feelings of inadequacy if they are unable to soothe their children.

- How do you feel when your child is crying?
- When is crying most triggering?
- Are there moments when their crying isn't as triggering?
- How do you respond when you are triggered by your child's crying?

Rule Breaking

If you've had to ask your child to do something more than once, you're not alone, and it doesn't mean you're a bad parent or have a bad kid. You're parenting an autonomous human, not a robot! We have to consider so many things when understanding why children break rules. Children's developmental stages play a role in their ability to follow rules. Likewise, children experience their own triggers and deal with their own challenging emotions, so it's not uncommon for rules to be broken, even in the most orderly household. We get it: humans don't always do what we want them to do! But being able to rationalize this may not make it any less frustrating if it is a trigger for you.

- How do you feel when your child is breaking a rule?
- When is rule breaking most triggering?
- Are there moments when their rule breaking isn't as triggering?
- How do you respond when you are triggered by this behavior?

Private Tantrums

Tantrums are the number one topic I discuss with my clients and yet a lot of parents assume their children are the only ones behaving this way. That, combined with the sheer difficulty of experiencing a child's tantrum, makes this a big trigger for a lot of parents. It can be so hard to keep calm and not match their explosions. It's so difficult to regulate our emotions during tantrums and yet our regulation is exactly what they need in order to return to calm.

- How do you feel when your child is throwing a tantrum?

- When is a tantrum most triggering?

- Are there moments when they throw a tantrum and it isn't as triggering?

- How do you respond when you are triggered by this behavior?

Public Tantrums

Very few experiences will humble you like the infamous grocery store tantrum. Picture the scene: your five-year-old is flailing on the floor and you are in a full-blown panic while a crowd of angry spectators judges the entire fiasco. Just kidding! Nobody really cares. But it sure as hell can feel like it sometimes. Sometimes when children experience big feelings in front of others, your ego can kick in. You may completely focus on how you look or how you think others are perceiving your parenting rather than focusing on the needs of your child. Maybe you feel helpless. Maybe you feel anxious or embarrassed. If this is your trigger, your feelings are still valid, even if they are completely self-focused. (Later, we'll explore managing your triggers so you can validate your own feelings while still meeting your child's needs moment by moment.)

- How do you feel when your child is throwing a tantrum in public?
- When is throwing a tantrum in public most triggering?
- Are there moments when their throwing a tantrum in public isn't as triggering?
- How do you respond when you are triggered by this behavior?

Being Touched

There can be very real and difficult reasons why you may not enjoy touch. Past experiences can make physical touch uncomfortable for some parents. You may be able to tolerate physical touch in some moments (like physical affection), while being unable to tolerate it in other instances (like during a tantrum).

This trigger is a lot to unpack and understand, and even thinking about it may bring up very big feelings. Like all triggers, it is not our goal to completely understand them or get rid of them altogether. Our awareness of our triggers and how we choose to respond to them has a greater impact than trying to completely eliminate them.

Consider a conversation I had with one of my clients. (We'll call her "Wanda.") Wanda told me that she absolutely cannot stand being touched when she's upset. And in true serendipitous fashion, the universe gave her a daughter who needs touch. This works out fine when only one of them is upset, but when both Wanda and her daughter are overwhelmed, they find themselves in a serious WTF moment.

Wanda asked, "What do I do? I feel so bad. I love her so much but I hate being touched. It makes my skin crawl." My response was something she probably didn't even consider: "It is actually okay that you don't want her to touch you."

We were corresponding via email, but I could imagine she was probably at least a bit confused. I reminded her that many of our triggers are out of our conscious control. She said being touched made her skin crawl. How the hell do you keep your skin from crawling? That's a journey that requires a lot of practice. Remember that any of the physical sensations we feel when we are triggered are automatic.

- How do you feel when you are touched?

- When is this most triggering?

- Are there moments when their touch isn't as triggering?

- How do you respond when you are triggered by this behavior?

Your Child Moving Slowly

Toddlers or turtles? That is the question! Turtles. That is the answer. They're freakin' turtles. Well, I can't speak for you, but mine move skillfully slow. Actually, I take that back. They move like normal humans, unless we have a time constraint. That's when the slow motion kicks in. Or worse—they all of a sudden have to do twenty-two cartwheels. Great!

If you can relate to this then you know how maddening it can be for their little batteries to start dying the minute you need to walk out the door. Their feet don't hurt. They don't need to bring all those toys. They aren't looking for their pet rock. They are stalling! Okay, so those are all unfair assumptions, but when I'm triggered it sure as hell feels personal. It's really important for me to recognize that though it *feels* like a personal attack, it's likely just a trigger.

- How do you feel when your child is moving slowly?

- When is this behavior most triggering?

- Are there moments when this isn't as triggering?
- How do you respond when you are triggered by this behavior?

Talking Back

I joke that my children can be spicier than ghost pepper wings dipped in wasabi! It's a joke, but it's pretty rooted in fact! I got in trouble for talking back as a child and I vowed to not be the kind of parent who punishes my children for expressing themselves. I thought I'd be able to hear my child get sassy and say, "Now, sweetie. You know we don't talk like that. Let's try again but a little bit nicer this time."

When she was a toddler, I was able to accept the ways she asserted herself; I was able to move through her sass gracefully and help her find different ways to communicate. But then she got older. She lost that baby voice, her sass revved up a bit, and I completely forgot my vow to myself. I started to get triggered. Thinking back, it's ironic that I had set up the conditions for my daughter to be able to express herself freely, but when she got to a certain age her exercising of that freedom of expression became one of my greatest triggers. Needless to say, I brought this upon myself! But the thing about triggers is they can often lie dormant. This is why it's important to have an ongoing awareness of your internal state. I'm constantly checking in with myself and examining how things make me feel.

- How do you feel when your child is talking back?
- When is back talk most triggering?
- Are there moments when their back talk isn't as triggering?
- How do you respond when you are triggered by their back talk?

Sibling Fighting

And then there were two! I imagined bringing my second child home and my oldest welcoming her with open arms. And that's exactly what happened. My firstborn absolutely loved her little sister. She would dress her up and play with her and hold her every chance she got. They built a very strong bond early, but as they grew older their friendship began to morph into a rivalry. All day long they would struggle with sharing, speaking kindly to each other, and respecting each other's space. The toddler even began hitting the oldest when she couldn't express her frustration verbally.

Sibling fighting can be a very difficult trigger to manage. Sibling fights can stir up conflicting feelings. You may feel a need to protect one child, while the other child may bring up feelings of anger and resentment. Managing these conflicting feelings can make it difficult to meet the needs of both children. In other moments where there is no clear aggressor, you may feel frustration toward both children, making it difficult to empathize with either of them.

- How do you feel when your children are fighting?
- When is sibling fighting most triggering?
- Are there moments when their fighting isn't as triggering?
- How do you respond when you are triggered by this behavior?

Your Child Is Struggling with a Task

Have you ever watched your child struggle to tie their shoes or complete a math assignment? Of course you have! Sometimes you may want to swoop in and save your child because it's so upsetting to watch them struggle. That's understandable but it may be keeping your child from growing into a confident and competent individual.

Some parents are able to sit with the discomfort of their children not succeeding, while others really struggle with it especially if it's something they feel the child "should" be able to do. I work with a lot of parents. And believe it or not, a lot of my clients feel embarrassment or anger when their kids struggle.

- How do you feel when your child is struggling with a task ?
- When is this most triggering?
- Are there moments when this isn't as triggering?
- How do you respond when you are triggered by this behavior?

Whining

Whining is a trigger that I hear about often from parents. It's difficult for some to manage the constant complaining. Maybe you can handle the first three "I hate the grocery store" complaints, but are you still calm after thirty minutes of your child moving slowly, rolling their eyes, and whining about how long you've been there? Of course, you want to help your child and meet their needs, but they don't *need* to leave the grocery store—they just *want* to leave. And that desire is completely imposing on your desire to cook dinner tonight! It's slowing down the process and overwhelming your thoughts. You explode: "Stop! It's not that serious. The more you complain, the longer it takes." But this doesn't help. They feel like you don't care; you feel like they don't care; and you are both utterly and completely... triggered.

- How do you feel when your child is whining?
- When is whining most triggering?
- Are there moments when whining isn't as triggering?
- How do you respond when you are triggered by their whining?

Developmentally Appropriate Mistakes

Whether you're changing the third pair of sheets this week or Googling how to get slime out of the carpet, these kinds of behaviors can be triggering. As our children grow and explore the world, they will inevitably make some mistakes that are, well, inconvenient. They just don't yet have the brain development or impulse control necessary to avoid certain behaviors. So when your curious three-year-old grabs a marker and starts drawing swirls on the wall, they probably aren't doing it to be disrespectful. They're just being a three-year-old! Still, you get triggered. Maybe you have company coming over soon. Maybe you just spent the day cleaning up and this is the last straw. So you react rather than respond: "Why would you do that? You know better. Give me that marker. You aren't allowed to use them anymore."

- How do you feel when your child is making mistakes?

- When is this most triggering?

- Are there moments when their developmentally appropriate mistakes aren't as triggering?

- How do you respond when you are triggered by these mistakes?

Inflexibility

Some children are less flexible than others. Maybe they freak out when it's time to leave the park or they have a meltdown at every little change in their day. You're managing everyone's needs, taking care of the home, and trying your best to have a smooth day. But their reactions to every little change in the environment are completely out of your control. Of course that can bring up a lot of emotions. Maybe you resort to force or coercion. Maybe you just shut down and let them take control of the day. Either way, inflexibility can be a major trigger for a lot of parents. Ask yourself these questions:

- How do you feel when your child is being inflexible?
- When is this behavior triggering?
- Are there moments when their inflexibility isn't as triggering?
- How do you respond when you are triggered by their inflexibility?

Of course, there are so many other things we could add to this list. Honestly, anything could be a trigger for you. So as you begin to notice more of your triggers, I encourage you to use these journal prompts to understand them a bit more:

- What is the triggering behavior?
- How do you feel when your child is exhibiting this behavior?
- When is this behavior most triggering?
- Are there moments when this behavior isn't as triggering?
- How do you respond when you are triggered by this behavior?

Using Emotional Regulation to Cope with Your Triggers

When we are able to recognize our triggers in the moment, we give ourselves the grace we need to regulate our way through them. The goal is not to live trigger-free, but to live less reactively. And you can do this through self-regulation. This is always my first step in the moments that require a bit more mental and emotional energy. When my toddler is throwing a tantrum, I regulate myself first. I have found that the more space I put between my child's actions and my reactions, the more likely I am to respond intentionally. When we're going to be late because we can't find the doll, I regulate myself first. When my oldest snaps back sarcastically, I make sure that I am first in a neutral, regulated state.

Of course, it's not something that comes naturally. Developing inner calm quite literally goes against our physiology for many of us. All of our basic needs really come down to one overarching human need: safety. As humans, security, moment by moment, is what fuels most of our emotions, thoughts, and behaviors. We are constantly oscillating between safety and stress, rest and reaction. Our nervous systems are broken down into two categories and they both respond to stress in different ways. First, our brains generate our flight, fight, freeze, or fawn response, and this is where most of us get stuck when we are triggered. This response is our brains telling us to respond as quickly as possible to preserve our safety. And no matter how much we evolve, we're still in many ways like the caveman whose heart began to beat faster when he heard the bushes rustling. Our fight-or-flight responses are activated just the same when we experience less life-threatening stimuli.

This response can be further heightened if safety was not consistently accessible to us in our childhoods. For many of us, fear and stress were normal parts of our day-to-day experiences. And so as children, our brains constantly picked up threat signals in our environments through a process called *neuroception*. Over time, this makes it difficult for your nervous system to detect safety, and this can result in a hypervigilance in our parenting, making our bodies respond disproportionately to the actual trigger. Your reactions to today's stressors can literally be the effect of how your brain has been conditioned to respond. In many ways, this is not your fault. When your child talks back, whines, hits, or doesn't clean their room, your autonomic nervous system is picking this up as a threat and responding with all of the previous data from years and years of stress and fear. Basically, your brain and body are just trying to keep you safe. So you don't have to beat yourself up if yelling or punishing seems to happen almost unconsciously. It'll only get in the way of your progress. And while it took years to condition this autonomic response, you can train your brain to recognize safety even when there is stress in your environment.

Dr. Steven Porges, author of *The Polyvagal Theory*, discovered the vagus nerve within our brains. A part of the parasympathetic nervous system, the vagus nerve oversees many bodily functions, one of which is mood regulation. With his polyvagal theory, Dr. Porges divided autonomic responses into three phases:

Social Engagement or Ventral Vagal: In this phase you are regulated and grounded. It's easy to access compassion, connection, and effective communication. It's much easier to get on your child's level, use a gentler tone, and be aware of your facial expressions in this state.

Mobilization or Fight-or-Flight: In this phase, your sympathetic nervous system is in control. This is the reactive state where you may yell, shame, blame, spank, or leave the situation altogether. Physically, you may be experiencing increased heart rate, chest tightening, shallow breaths, or muscle tension.

Immobilization or Dorsal Vagal: This is the shutdown or freeze state. When you are in this state, you may experience a decrease in heart rate, facial expressions, or depth of breath; have difficulty making eye contact; or experience numbness.

These states are often described as the "Polyvagal Ladder" with Social Engagement being at the top. These states are involuntary and conditioned but with practice, you can learn to support yourself in moving up that ladder. If your typical response is to completely shut down, you can learn what helps you move up into fight-or-flight and then back to social engagement. If you are a yeller, you can learn how to move from mobilization to social engagement. You don't have to completely stop being triggered in order to respond to your child more intentionally. You just have to train your brain to move into a state of safety and security before you respond. And

6 How to Not Lose Your Shit

that is very possible. The more connected you become with your nervous system, the more access you will have to conscious choice when you're triggered. And you build that connection through paying attention to your physical responses to your triggers.

You may be saying to yourself, "Okay, Destini. That was a lot. What the heck are you talking about?" Basically, what I'm saying is that the better you get at noticing the changes in your body when you're triggered, the easier it will be to respond rather than react. In order to do this, first recognize how the trigger is impacting you physically. Next, ask yourself how you can move into the next highest state on the ladder.

If you are shut down (dorsal vagal), how can you gently move into fight-or-flight? Fight-or-flight isn't the most favorable state, but you won't be able to return to the top of the ladder without going there first. So if you're immobilized, how can you mobilize? What activity can you do? It can literally be anything, just so long as long as it's not harmful, of course. Sometimes when I'm shut down I use this as an opportunity to clean or go for a walk. While I'm doing an activity, I'll typically move into fight-or-flight. I might get really angry or frustrated thinking about the situation. Again, that's normal because you don't just jump from shut down to social engagement. Once I've gotten to the fight-or-flight state, I can then find a calming tool to bring myself back to "safety." For me, that tool might be deep breathing, visualizing, EFT tapping, massaging my neck and shoulders, a nap, affirmations, or a snack. Once I'm calm and enter into the social engagement state, I can then proceed rationally and decide whether to ignore, manage, or address my child's behavior. There's a saying in positive discipline: "Connect before you correct." And it advises the parent to connect with their child before they go into problem solving or discipline. I love this saying, but I think it's missing one important piece of the puzzle—connect with yourself first. Regulate your own nervous system first!

Now I know this seems like a heavy process. And that's because it is. This takes time and you won't often have that kind of time when you're in the grocery store or in the drop-off line at school. But there will be so many moments where you will have time to attend to your physical responses before you react to your child's behavior. We're not always in a rush. Those moments are where you build these skills so that when you get triggered, you can have fewer dorsal state moments and spend less time in fight-or-flight.

Part 2

The Four Cs of Intentional Parenting

Take a second to ground yourself before we move on to this next section of the book.

Inhale. Exhale. Take a deep breath. If you can, close your eyes and connect with your body. Wiggle your hands and fingers. Rotate your neck, reach up, stretch out. Now take a second to be still.

How do you feel?

I hope you feel open and calm. I hope you feel receptive, because I'm about to share the culmination of everything that I have consumed along my parenting journey. The following chapters are *the work*, and probably the reason you picked this book up in the first place! It's time to dive into what intentional parenting actually looks like. I'm going to outline what life can be like for your family once you've taken radical responsibility. It's the nitty-gritty of how to respond to the many challenges you will inevitably face in your home.

I could spend this entire book encouraging you to take responsibility for yourself and helping you increase your self-awareness. But I believe I'd be doing you a disservice if I didn't also give you tools to support the journey that we started in the first part of this book. And while your family dynamics will look completely different than mine, there are several tools and techniques that you can add to your tool belt that you can lean on in your parenting journey. The more tools you have, the less likely you are to fall back on habitual patterns that do not serve you or your family. The more you practice, the more automatic intentional parenting becomes. Just like with our children, repetition is what makes information stick. It's how we learn. It's how we create new connections in the brain and form new habits.

Principles are everything in intentional parenting! But greater than any one strategy is the principle behind it. The principles are what will allow you to come up with your own positive parenting solutions. So over the next four chapters, you'll learn about the Four Cs of Intentional Parenting.

7

Connection
(Prioritizing the Relationship)

Relationships are complicated. Why? Because people are complicated. Relationships take work, time, and constant flexibility. There's no single secret ingredient that makes a healthy relationship, and this is especially true in the parent-child dynamic. Sometimes you can feel like you're crushing it and other days it can feel like you've never parented before in your life. You'll always find yourself constantly changing and adapting. What works in one moment may not work in another; there's no magic tool to fix all of the problems that arise from day to day. But I can say there has been one dependable principle in my household that at least *feels* like magic. This one principle is *connection*, and it's the foundation of my parenting style. It sets the tone for everything that occurs in my home.

What Happens When We Lack Connection?

A lack of connection can impact even the smallest day-to-day things. Oftentimes, when children feel unseen or disempowered, they will act out. Don't be fooled by the sass or the tantrums.

Our kids have an innate desire to collaborate with us and contribute. But when they feel like their feelings and desires don't matter, that can all go out the window. But is that really surprising? If I'm in a relationship, in a friendship, or on a team, and my feelings, thoughts, and opinions are constantly being ignored or shut down, I can feel small. I can recall relationships when the participants didn't take the time to build and sustain a positive rapport with me and as a result it was a lot more difficult to be collaborative with them. Many relationships and partnerships end because other things are prioritized over connection. People often skip over the importance of building rapport and go right into problem solving and collaboration. Who has time to connect? We've got deadlines and tasks to complete, right? But then we're blindsided when things inevitably get thrown off track and we go into the never-ending cycle of finding and fixing the symptoms of a much bigger problem. What many people don't realize is that the root cause of these issues is typically just cracks in the foundation. And that foundation is safety and connection, which is the root of trust, respect, and consideration in a healthy relationship. It's how we set and honor boundaries, effectively work together, and ultimately enjoy the relational experience.

So how do you begin the process of building the foundation of an intentional relationship with your child? Through intimacy. We all have this innate desire to be loved and connected with others. That's a major part of being a human being. Whether your child is an introvert or an extrovert, they need some level of intimacy with you. But when that intimacy is disturbed or ignored, their sense of security can be disrupted. And guess what happens when kids don't feel secure in their environments? It's the same thing that happens when adults don't feel safe—they begin to react rather than respond; they assert themselves in inappropriate ways; they completely shut down or overreact; they panic and exhibit their anxiety in their own individual ways. All of these responses can completely throw off the vibe in the house.

Creating Connection in My Home

I've personally seen the impact connection-focused parenting can have and it's amazing how quickly I can shift things with a little intentional intimacy. Connection is the place where I always begin when I'm helping other parents get to the root of some of their most challenging moments. And it's also what I always come back to when something is off for me and my children. My connection with my kids comes before discipline. It comes before routines and schedules. It comes before teaching and instructing. It is blended and meshed into everything we do. Though we have many goals and values in our home, connection is the one thing that I prioritize most. When we are connected, the day flows a bit easier, moments are a bit more meaningful, and I am not reaching for a wine bottle by 6:00 p.m.! My kids feel safer when we prioritize connection. I feel more rooted and intentional in my parenting when we prioritize connection. Basically, it's the pixie dust I sprinkle over the shit show to keep us, and oftentimes get us, back on track.

Sometimes we just have off weeks in my house. During those weeks nothing seems to be flowing right for my kiddos. My daughters are more combative than usual; they can't seem to get on the same page and every little thing ignites a tantrum. Similarly, my days seem to be a little more chaotic. I keep missing deadlines and losing keys. I'm easily triggered and edgy. And my self-care meter is close to zero. During those weeks, it's hard to remember that it's not always that chaotic, and as a result it's very easy to spiral. But the longer I ruminate on what's not working, the harder it is to shift to a more positive space.

Now I'd be lying if I said my first instinct is always to immediately jump up and start using my tools. Most times it takes a few days for me to realize that we need a reset. And if I'm being honest, there have been moments where it has taken significantly longer, but the better I get at noticing when things are off, the more efficient I get at repairing them. So after I've banged my head against the wall for a day—or seven—I come back to that radical responsibility I first talked about at the beginning of the book. I first make sure that I'm present and connected to myself. I check in with how I'm taking care of myself and I remind myself that my external world is just a reflection of my own internal world.

I remind myself that when my kids feel safe and connected and securely attached to me, their behaviors change and our relationships change. I can change the course of our day with connection. I can change the course of our weeks, months, and years with connection. It will always be number one in my parenting toolbox. Without it, there's pure chaos in my home. With it, there is openness, kindness, respect, growth, and peace.

Tools for Creating Connection

So now you know the importance of focusing on connection. But how do you actually do that? Well, I'm going to share some of the tools I use in my home, but ultimately it's going to be up to you and your child to figure out what builds intimacy and trust. Does creating connection just mean playing with your kids all day? Does helping them feel seen and heard mean ignoring your own desires and needs? Do you have to spend a lot of time and money to make it happen? No, no, and *heck* no!

Connection is flexible. There are no "have-tos" in building your connection with your child. Will you play with your child sometimes? I sure hope so. Will you sometimes choose to meet your child's needs before you meet your own? You know the answer to that question—of course you will. Healthy relationships sometimes require a certain level of sacrifice and compromise. And can you spend money or get wrapped up in a free activity with your child for hours? You sure can!

You get to decide what works for your family. Your home is unique and every child is different. So flexibility is actually really important when you begin to focus on connection. One child may love deep conversations while the other may just want to be silent in the room with you. Both are opportunities for connection. And just like every child is different, every day is different. Some days your child may really love playing with Legos, and then on a random Tuesday they may declare Legos to be the most boring toy on the planet. Be flexible and be consistent! The more you prioritize being present with your child, the more opportunities you'll find to connect with them.

Showing Compassion

Can you sit with your child's feelings without feeling like you need to "fix" them? Can you witness your child make mistakes without shaming them or feeling ashamed yourself? Can you show sympathy even if you don't think their problems are a "big deal"? This can have a huge impact on their sense of identity and their self-esteem. As you give them the opportunity to think, feel, and mess up, they will feel more connected and comfortable with you. As a result, it can become much easier for them to make empowered choices that positively impact the family.

Take a moment to think about your closest friend or family member. This is the person who you go to when you need help or support. This is the person who encourages you when you're sad or reminds you of your awesomeness whenever you forget. When you make a mistake, you feel safe sharing it with that person. You know they will hold you accountable in a way that doesn't demean or disrespect you. Now think of the total opposite person. Many of us have, or have had, someone in our lives who we would not consider a "safe space." Think about what happens any time you make a mistake. Do they lecture you, focus on blame, or bring up past mistakes? Do they invalidate your feelings by saying things like "you shouldn't be upset" or "it's not that big of a deal"? Most times we only interact in those relationships out of feelings of obligation or habit. What I want to point out is if we do choose to interact with these kinds of people, it's not because we feel deeply connected to them.

I want to be in that first kind of relationship with my kids. I want them to know that I am attuned and present with them enough to give them whatever they need, emotionally or mentally, in the moment. If my child needs to cry, that's okay. If my child needs a hug, that's okay. If my child makes a mistake, I can choose to empower her rather than criticize her. I can remind my daughters that everyone makes mistakes and that it's completely normal to have a harder time with some things than with others. I can try my hardest to show my children compassion even in their challenges. Basically I can give my children the support they need. Support can be described as acceptance of your child's experience and confidence in their ability to get through it. Building intimacy through our support is not about fixing things for our children and constantly accommodating them. It's about reminding them that you care about their feelings and experiences and you believe in your heart that they can do hard things. Not only does this help your children feel connected to you, it also helps them feel connected to themselves.

Sometimes I miss the mark, but it's what I strive for, but that doesn't mean there aren't times when it's hard for me to be compassionate. Have you ever gotten a cup thrown at your head? I have! Have you ever gotten an award for being the worst mom ever? I have! In those moments, it's extremely hard for me to be compassionate and understanding.

It may also be easier to show compassion to one child than it is to another. Your temperament may mesh better with one child than another. Maybe that child triggers you less. Maybe they are at an age where it's easier for you to work with them. For me, compassion has been easier at different stages of my daughter's developmental stages. (To be honest: compassion was a lot easier to achieve in the toddler stage. I could kiss a boo-boo without even thinking about it. I could pick my daughter up when she was scared, without trying to force her to be brave. But I've also recognized that as she's gotten older, it's become more difficult for me to have compassion.)

7 Connection

The truth is that sometimes my daughter's big problems don't feel big for me. That internal alarm doesn't always go off for me as readily as it did when she fell off her bike at five years old. And in those moments when I am stressed about my own "grownup" problems, I sometimes forget that her problems feel just as big to her as mine do to me. It could feel like the end of the world for her to lose a friend or the remote to a favorite toy. And I can't expect her nine-year-old brain to process disappointment the same way a healthy adult brain can. Likewise, I can't force myself to care about losing a video game the same way she does. But I do care deeply about *her*. And I don't have to feel exactly what she feels in order to care. And so in those moments, I have to remind myself that her feelings are valid and that if she needs me it is my honored job as her parent to show up for her. Even when I don't "get it." Even when she's being sassy, disagreeing with me, making a mistake, or having a hard time with big feelings and being sassy or unkind to her younger sister. I have to remind myself that I can discipline, teach, and encourage her in ways that don't make her feel small or disempowered. In any situation, if I dismiss or even try to fix her feelings, I'm not going to make her feel empowered to make better decisions or manage her emotions better in the future. And so I'm constantly reminding myself to see the best in her, even in the moments when she's behaving in a way that is challenging for me.

I'd like to share a helpful tool I use to strengthen my compassion, which I learned in my program at the Jai Institute for Parenting. The next time you are struggling to have compassion for your child, try to visualize your child in the future. Imagine them as a thirty-five-year-old adult and then, in your mind, ask them these questions and then mentally answer them as your child's thirty-five-year-old self:

- What do you need?
- How can I help you?
- What is happening?
- How are you feeling?

This is a great exercise because a lot of times compassion is difficult to achieve simply because your child may not be expressing their feelings in a way that is easy for you to handle or even understand. Some kids shut down while others share their emotions through tantrums, yelling, hitting, and other behaviors. Sometimes kids have a difficult time finding the words to tell you what they're really feeling. At other times, they may ramble off every thought or feeling that comes to mind. In both cases, if you are struggling to find compassion, take a moment to visualize what your child might be trying to express beneath the irrational reaction.

This exercise can be extremely helpful. Quite often it can be difficult for us to be compassionate toward an underlying problem because sometimes the symptoms of the problem are triggering to us, right? So when the toddler is screaming because they can't get a piece of candy and they're triggered, it may be difficult for you to relate to the underlying need. Being tired or running late or just having an argument with your mother-in-law can make things even worse. And you can pretty much forget about compassion being your immediate response. But if you freeze and imagine your child as a rational adult with reasoning and regulating capacities, what might they share with you? Maybe it would sound something like, "I'm feeling like all I've heard all day is 'no.' And this piece of candy would make me so, so happy because it feels like I never get what I want. And it feels like the people around me always get what they want, but I don't. It just seems really unfair that I don't have as much control over my choices as the big people." You can then come back to the moment and see that even our children have very real and very understandable desires underneath all their tantrums. By performing this exercise, you often can get to the root problem rather than just trying to manage the symptoms of the problem.

Now, does that mean you give them that piece of candy? Probably not. But what it does mean is that you can respond to them in a way that is caring and understanding. Rather than shutting down the tantrum, which is dealing with the symptom, you can speak to the underlying need. "I know it's hard to hear 'no.' That can be really frustrating." That is compassion. It doesn't mean you give in. It just means you have genuine concern for your children's emotions.

Of course there will be moments when you do lean toward flexibility. "Now I know that it's hard to hear, but no, you can't have the candy right now. Mommy will buy it for you and we'll have it after dinner." Or maybe you change your mind completely and you say to yourself, "You know what? She had a rough day at daycare. She fell and bumped her head. I said 'no' to literally the last twenty things she asked me, so maybe I do have space for a 'yes.'" Would this teach her that tantrums are how you get candy? Maybe, but I doubt it. Especially if you practice the discipline strategies outlined in future chapters on a consistent basis. If you sympathize with your child and connect their feelings (not their behaviors) to why you said "yes," I'm willing to bet you'll teach them a much greater lesson. If you respond with "You've heard 'no' so much today. That must be tough. I can say 'yes' to the candy. I love you," then they may learn one of the kindest lessons we can teach them: that their parent cares about their desires and their feelings are safe with them. I can't say for sure what would be the right approach to follow in this kind of situation—every moment, child, and parent are different—but I can say that if you are making a decision with your child that is rooted in compassion, you can't get it wrong.

Growing Together

Another way to connect with your child is by growing together. There is something to be said about the process of failing and then triumphing with another person. You see these kinds of bonds in the military, with fraternities and sororities, in career partnerships, and in other long-term relationships. There is a deep bond that is developed through the shared completion of a challenging task. Likewise, incorporating shared challenges into the parent-child relationship can be really beneficial for creating connections. It's also an opportunity to strengthen your child's growth mindset. When people feel comfortable making mistakes, they become more confident learners. As a result, the process of discipline is so much easier and, in a lot of cases, unnecessary.

If you have not been trying new things or if you have gotten into a complacent funk, why not try something new with your child? Maybe there's a martial arts class at the local recreation center. Or you've always wanted to learn coding and your child has an interest in that as well. Why not take a class together? Maybe you both can go to the gym together. Maybe you can get into baking, hiking, or knitting. Trying new things with your child strips away hierarchy and strict roles and gives you both the opportunity to see each other grow. It's just the two of you meeting a challenge. And as you struggle (like we all do with new things), it can offer the opportunity for you to model problem solving, strategizing, and overcoming obstacles.

I think one of the most beautiful things about focusing on connection is that it allows us to walk alongside this journey of life with our kids. It allows us to really see them but it also allows them to see us, as well. We get to become the Yoda that guides them, rather than the forceful authoritarian. When we do life with our children, they connect with us in a way that builds trust. And the more they trust us and their environment, the more open they will be to contributing and cooperating. So go ahead, put this book down for a few minutes and go sign yourself and your child up for that community art class that keeps popping up on your social media feed.

Play

My next suggestion for connecting with your child is through play. I have found play to be extremely challenging for a lot of parents. We have serious jobs and serious relationships and serious bills. So, for a lot of us, it can feel uncomfortable to make time for play. By no means do I want to belittle anyone's circumstances. I know a lot of us are in survival mode and I can completely empathize with that. And I understand that if financial or environmental safety or mental

7 Connection

safety are compromised, it can be very difficult to show up for your kids in a playful way. If that is the case, make returning to security a priority. Remember that everything starts with you. If you don't feel secure, it will be extremely hard to provide that feeling of security to your children. Prioritize your emotional, environmental, and mental safety so that you can get to a place where play with your children is a bit more accessible. If you are not in survival mode and play is still getting placed on the back burner because of the daily to-do list, I would invite you to think about how much time you spend yelling and repeating yourself. Think about all the social media scrolling or Netflix bingeing. Think about how many emails could have waited until the morning. And then ask yourself if you really don't have time to play. Chances are there is at least a small window of time available to engage in play with your children.

What isn't typically available to a lot of parents is energy. This goes back to self-care and prioritizing things that don't drain your energy so that lighthearted things like play don't feel like such a chore. In the beginning, when parents are opening up to the idea of play, I like to encourage them to first just try to find small consistent moments of play. You wouldn't lift a hundred pound dumbbell on your first visit to a gym. Likewise, committing to an hour of imaginative play each day can feel like you're lifting a hundred pounds if you haven't prioritized play in the past. Start small and find a type of play that doesn't feel disingenuous. Play has so many different forms. If playing with dolls seems unrealistic for you right now, there are other ways to play! So many people overcomplicate play and make it way more complex than it needs to be. For smaller children play can be pretty much anything. It's all about exploring their environment. Letting them run their hands in a bowl of flour while you cook and interact with them is play. Popping bubbles one at a time in the tub is play. As they get older and more social, play becomes whatever they like to do with their peers. This can make things a little more tricky, but there is always something you can give a little of your attuned attention to! For example, my daughter loves to play video games. She would play on her computer with her friends all day long if she could.

I, however, am not the biggest fan. But I made it a priority to find a game that we can both enjoy together sometimes. And the more we play, the more I get to know her. And the more I get to know her, the more things we find in common. This useful information helps me find more activities for us to do together. You'd be surprised how magical it can be for your child to spend time with you doing things they enjoy. And as you build playfulness in your relationship, something amazing will start to happen. You'll start to recognize how much more connected, lighthearted, and playful you are in your discipline. And that makes it much easier to stay away from punitive, shame-based techniques.

Special Time

One of my favorite tools to use for increasing your consistency with "play" is *special time*. (I borrowed this technique from Dr. Laura Markham, who suggested designating a specific one-on-one time that is set aside just for you and your child.)

Special time can have so many benefits:

- It can strengthen a child's sense of security and connection to their parent.
- It gives the child the parent's present and attuned attention.
- It opens up the floor for communication about difficult topics, like their "big feelings."
- It strengthens a parent's ability to understand, relate to, and connect with their child.
- It encourages trust between the parent and the child.

Special time gives you the opportunity to intentionally strengthen your relationship with your child. When done correctly, you can help your child meet their need for play and connection.

7 Connection

And the only way that you can make sure that it's effective and that you don't miss the mark is if you take your hands off the wheel and let your child lead the moment. When we're practicing special time in my house, I only offer input when it's requested or when it's absolutely necessary. I don't use this time to ask a bunch of questions or dictate every little detail. If you get easily triggered by things like your child getting a new piece of paper after only drawing two dots, you are not alone—I can't stand it! And if you can't stand the thought of Barbie wearing pajamas to the pool party, I totally get it! It's nonsensical and I'm sure you might want to step in with a much more reasonable outfit. But don't do it! Just let Barbie be supremely overdressed. Over time, it will get easier to let your child be in control during special time. The more time you spend letting your child be in the driver's seat, the more comfortable you'll be with this kind of child-led play. And that's good for you and your child! It shows them that they can handle some responsibility, and you can handle some direction, which in many homes is a complete dynamic shift! (You can find more benefits to special time at ahaparenting.com.)

Letting your child be in the driver's seat may mean saying "yes" to something that your child may not typically get to do. For instance, if there are toys in the house that are off limits to the younger child, then your oldest may only get to use them while alone in their room. Maybe you typically say, "Yes, you can use the markers. Take them to your room so your sister doesn't get into them." But during special time you get the opportunity to use those markers together. Or maybe you use special time to say "yes" to something that your children can only do with your supervision. Sometimes my daughter and I use special time to watch social media videos. She's not allowed to use these apps any other time; however, we can watch the videos together and I can scroll past things I find harmful or inappropriate. Now, Dr. Markham wouldn't necessarily be a proponent of this approach as she believes that special time should be unstructured. She likely would recommend avoiding things like video games and watching videos because it doesn't leave as much room for communication and imagination. But I think it's important to be tuned into the child's individual needs.

My oldest was homeschooled, so we always spent time together. So much of our day was just she and I being present with each other. We were always creating, thinking critically, and communicating together. But quite often when we had special time her desire would be to do the complete opposite and she would want to turn that part of her brain off and just laugh or connect in a more physical way, like sitting on my lap while playing a video game or snuggling up and reading her favorite book series. Even with video games or books, we would still have conversations and communicate. She would share what made her laugh or what she thought would happen next in a book. On the other hand, my four-year-old was in daycare. She had structured activities all day long and she was away from me for much of the day, so we really didn't have as many opportunities to connect, communicate, and be imaginative together. She typically would choose to do something like building with blocks, having a tea party, or going outside and playing tag. With both children, it was important for me to use special time to focus on whatever they were needing in the moment. And I would do that by letting them choose every single detail. I didn't suggest we read a book on the couch or go outside to play tag. Instead, they got to be in control. Their job was to define both the "what" and the "how." My job was to define the "when" and for how long. If my toddler wanted to high-five for twenty minutes, that's what we were going to do!

Here are some steps you can take to incorporate special time in your home:

1. **Schedule it.** Choose a time you can easily commit to. It may not be every day. If you have multiple kids, maybe you rotate. The important thing is to be intentional about making it a regular occurrence. Dr. Markham recommends choosing a time where the other child is sure to not interrupt. I have found that scheduling special time

increases its priority level. Connection is way too important to leave to chance, so if I can schedule a meeting for work, I certainly can schedule our special time.

2. **Create clear expectations.** The beauty of intentional special time is that you can make it consistent. However, without introducing limits, it can become hard to keep up with it. Remember: you get to decide the time and duration. Letting your child know when special time will take place and how long it will be gives them something to expect on a consistent basis. Rather than telling them you'll play later, you can let them know that Monday, Wednesday, and Thursday afternoons are their times to get fifteen minutes of your undivided attention. Now, some of you may read those specific days and think "Oh my, this is a commitment." And that's because it is. Make the expectations clear so that you can be accountable for prioritizing this time.

3. **Set a timer.** Timers are great visual cues for children and help them get used to transitions. It doesn't mean they won't get upset when special time is over, but over time using a timer can help children get used to time limitations.

4. **Give them the lead.** Tell your child they are in charge. Again, they get to decide the "what" and "how."

5. **Listen and learn.** Take the opportunity to practice active listening. Don't overpower the conversations. Instead, show up to special time with the intention of learning rather than teaching. Let it be an opportunity to learn about your child's feelings, thoughts, opinions, and imagination.

6. **Use transitions to end the moment.** Ending special time is probably going to suck for your child. They'd play all day if they could, but transitions can make handling these time limitations a bit easier. Try using a fun transition, like pretending you both are rocket ships blasting off into another room to help them move into the rest of

the day. You can choose a song to play as you dance back into the common area. You can create a secret handshake to conclude special time. Get creative and come up with something that works with you and your child. I made up a quick song when my daughter was four and we still use it at the end of special time: "Special time was so much fun. It kinda sucks that it's done. But special time comes every day. So we'll be back to sit and play."

Like I said at the beginning of the chapter, connection sort of feels like magic. Every time I recommend connection tools like special time to parents in my community, it's amazing how quickly they see changes in their children's behaviors. And that's why I focused this chapter on connection—I believe that it is the ultimate foundation for positive parenting. If you start anywhere else you will have a much harder time with positive discipline. Without connection, we can completely miss the point of this amazing and complex opportunity that we have in being their parents.

8

Curiosity
(Seeking to Understand)

"I hate you."

What would your first thought be if your child said those words to you? Or if this isn't new territory, what *was* your first thought? "How dare she say that! After all I've done for her?!" Or was it, "OMG, my child really does hate me. I'm failing." If your first thought was close to either of those, I want you to know that that's normal as hell.

You, like many other parents, may personalize your child's behavior in some way if you parent without intention, and you may struggle to see yourself as separate from the child's behavior. When your children fail, make a mistake, have a tantrum, or act out, you may feel a heightened level of responsibility for their actions. Likewise, some parents may struggle to see their children as separate from the behaviors. So, when their children say things like, "I hate you," they may see their children as bad, sensitive, disrespectful... the list goes on. And they often might come to one of two conclusions—either they are broken or their children are broken:

"If my child is bad, I need to fix my child. I mean, God forbid I raise a bad child who turns into this awful, cruel adult. No, no, no! I need to put a stop to this now!"

"If my child hates me, I must be failing. I don't know what to do. No matter how hard I try, I'm terrible at this."

What kind of discipline do you think would result from these kinds of narratives? In both of these instances, the discipline that follows will often be fear- and anxiety-based. I imagine harsh punishments or yelling. I can also imagine a parent melting into their own shame and quickly trying to fix their child's feelings: "Oh, no. Okay, Mommy is sorry. Here, you can have the candy."

The parent will most likely go for whatever reactive option would quickly ease the anxiety of raising a "bad person" or being a "bad parent." We are often unconscious to how these narratives are directing our choices with discipline, but they can show up any time our children display challenging behaviors. When your child cries at the smallest issue, an unconscious response seen through the lens of your child being flawed may be "Oh no, I'm raising an overly sensitive child." When your child empties a bag of potato chips in the middle of the grocery store, an unconscious belief that sees yourself as flawed may be "Oh no, I look like a terrible parent."

As we grow in our intentionality, it's important that we stand firm in the belief that both we and our children are separate from our behaviors. We can learn to recognize that when our children act out, it is a symptom of what they are experiencing and *not* a symptom of who they are. The same goes for you. When your child acts out, it is a symptom of your experience with your child, not an indication of the kind of parent you are. Seen from that vantage point, you can see that neither you nor your child needs "fixing," there is simply a problem that needs solving. Or, better put, there is an experience that needs to be understood and integrated in a healthier way.

We are here to help our children with their experiences. Their struggles are an opportunity for us to learn more about what they need and how we can support them. And remember, support is just the combination of acceptance and confidence. When they have a tantrum, they need support for their experience of pain or discomfort, not criticism. When they can't sit still at the dinner table, they need support for their overstimulation, not a punishment. When they say "I hate you," they need to feel safe, and they need support with articulating their underlying emotions. Our children need us to support them over and over in order to learn the behaviors we are trying to teach them. Where many parents get tripped up is in using the most appropriate kind of support for the moment. When the help is fear-based, there's a sense of urgency that may cause a parent to jump to quick solutions (fight, flight, freeze, fawn). But you can miss so much valuable information when you respond impulsively. Think of it this way: Pepto Bismol may be a great choice if you're experiencing an upset stomach, but it can actually be harmful if that upset stomach you're experiencing is because you're pregnant. A doctor wouldn't suggest using it without a proper understanding of the situation. Likewise, it can be harmful to jump to quick fixes for your children's behavioral symptoms without first getting curious about the underlying causes.

Finding Curiosity

So how do you give your children the help they need? How do you know how to respond? This is where the second of the Four Cs of Intentional Parenting comes into play. If you want to avoid reactive discipline, you have to use the principle of *curiosity*. You have to practice seeking to understand before you act. (I said *practice* because moving into curiosity takes consistency and daily practical application.) It can feel foreign to look beneath your child's behavior and ask questions *before* you react, but that's exactly what I'm suggesting you try. When you lead with curiosity, you give yourself an opportunity to make level-headed decisions that honor your children.

Getting curious about your child's behavior is about letting them "off the hook." Yes, you read that right. That may sound crazy, but I'd like to challenge the idea that our children need to be "on the hook" in the first place. This kind of thinking just pits us against our children and creates a space that breeds punitive discipline. You have an incredible child. You don't need to change them! So, let *them* off the hook and instead focus on what's beneath their *behavior.* Allow them to not be the problem or the bad child. Give them grace and believe the truth of who they really are. You'll still be able to teach your child how to clean their room or use kind language. They'll still learn boundaries and independence and all the things you want to teach them. But they'll learn them from someone who believes that they are inherently good: you. When you remember the principle of curiosity, you can show up more appropriately for whatever your child needs in the moment. Curiosity lets you get to the heart of the issue. It puts fear and anxiety to the side and sets the foundation for effective, compassionate teaching. It allows you to release the personalization of the behavior and the urge to "fix it." Curiosity allows you to show up where your child is and give them the most effective guidance you can.

Who, What, and When

You can practice the principle of curiosity by asking the three Ws: *who, what, and when.*

Who

Your two-year-old son is throwing cereal on the floor… again. You're frustrated, but you bend down, pick up the cereal, and put it in the trash. You head over to the high chair, get close to your child, and in a calm voice whisper, "Sweetie, cereal does not belong on the

8 Curiosity

floor. Let's try again." Of course it's annoying, but you react gently because you understand that he's two years old. He's learning. No need to panic.

Now let's fast-forward. He's now nine years old and no matter what you say you can't quite get him to clean up after himself. After a long day at work, you walk into his room and see clothes, shoes, papers, and even food on the floor. Without even thinking you scold him and say, "What's the matter with you? Clean this up!" You leave him to it and return an hour later to find that either the room looks exactly the same or it's still not even close to being up to your standards. Now you've had it! Instantly and unconsciously, you feel the emotional weight of raising a "lazy" child. And so you scream at the top of your lungs, "That! Is! It! Clean it up right freakin' now!" Why? What happened to the calm voice you had when he was a toddler? What happened to making a gentle request? Well, one major thing changed—your expectations. Your expectations for a nine-year-old are not the same as your expectations for a toddler. And for good reason (sort of). In most cases, a nine-year-old can do far more than a toddler. The problem is you may not be as aware of what to expect from a toddler versus what to realistically expect from an older child. What exactly *can* your nine-year-old do? And is consistent, adequate room cleaning a matter of "won't" or "can't"? Do you actually know if being able to clean their room the first time you ask, and doing so in a pristine way that meets your standards, is developmentally appropriate for your child? Well, what if I told you it isn't? You might be shocked to learn that most nine-year-olds' brains still struggle with simple tasks like cleaning their rooms. In fact, executive functioning doesn't even fully develop until adulthood. That means that things like starting tasks, planning, prioritizing, and organization are difficult for most children. And you need all of those skills to clean a room. And you damn sure need them to clean it well! If I told an adult to clean their room, their brain might say the following:

"Okay, let me get up... " (Starting tasks)

"... I'm going to pick up everything off the floor, make the bed, vacuum, and dust..." (Planning)

"... I'll start with my clothes on the floor since that's the hardest task..." (Prioritizing)

"... I'll put my socks in this drawer, hang my pants, and fold my shirts." (Organization)

And they'd do that almost automatically. Why? Because their executive functioning is more developed than a child's. But what would happen if I asked a child whose executive functioning isn't developed yet to clean their room? They'd probably think this:

"I'll clean my room..."

"... Oh snap, there's a new episode of my favorite show..." (Difficulty starting tasks)

"... Okay, the episode's over, but this room is just way too messy. How am I going to clean it up?..." (Difficulty planning)

"... And what do I even do first?..." (Difficulty prioritizing)

"... How does my mom make my closet make sense?" (Difficulty organizing)

You see, it's really not that your child won't straighten their room or clean it to your standards, it's that they probably do not have the brain development to do so on a consistent basis. And so that leaves you with two options: 1) accept where they are and choose and support them as they grow this skill, or 2) force the premature progression of their development and choose a punitive approach. The first option keeps your connection intact and fosters their growth in a healthy way. Unfortunately, most of us don't have an abundance of education on brain development. If you haven't got a clue, don't feel bad. I'm no scientist. Can I list every appropriate behavior for every developmental stage off the top of my head? I certainly cannot. So what are you to do? The good news is that you don't have to be an expert in developmental psychology. You just have to be an intentional parent. For me, that means that when I come up against a difficult behavior, I choose to investigate whether that behavior is developmentally appropriate before I choose my discipline strategy. If a behavior isn't developmentally appropriate, I take it as a sign that I may need more information or resources to support my child. But if something is developmentally appropriate, it's usually an indication that I just need to relax and choose a developmentally appropriate discipline strategy. When my preschooler started throwing a tantrum every morning at school drop-off, I got curious about whether this kind of separation anxiety was appropriate. When I found out that it was, I was able to gently support her through that developmental stage rather than forcing her to get comfortable doing something she wasn't developmentally ready to do. You can follow the same approach in your parenting. The next time your child spits or starts dropping F-bombs at church, you can pause before you freak out and then ask yourself if how they are acting is aligned with where they are in relation to their development. This will help you make sound, rational decisions about how to support them. Leaning on developmental appropriateness when we face challenging behaviors is a very fair and logical place to start practicing curiosity. You may not have time to read full-blown research articles and thumb through empirical data—I'm not expecting you to become a psychologist—but there are some really practical ways to find out if your child's behavior is appropriate. Here's what I do when I'm trying to figure out what's going on with my kids:

1. **I ask my therapist.** You know why I love my therapist so much? Because she's smarter than me. At least she is when it comes to the brain. So, anytime I have a question about my child's development, I ask her. If you have a therapist who you trust, especially one who's well-versed in developmental psychology, you should use that resource.

2. **I call a trusted friend.** If you don't have access to a
therapist, the next best thing can be a trusted friend.
When's the last time you had an honest conversation
with another parent? Many of us are afraid to share the
difficult behaviors our children are exhibiting, but it can
actually be a really helpful step in understanding our own
children's behaviors. Some of the craziest things I've heard
from other parents are actually pretty consistent across
the board. One mom told me that her preteen kept peeing
in bottles and leaving them in his room. (I apologize for
the graphic description, but I'm sharing it because this is
the kind of "crazy" stuff I hear! And if you're being honest
about your parenting journey, I know you've faced some
stuff you couldn't have ever imagined.) Now back to the
bottles. It turns out it's actually not that crazy. Literally a
week after talking to the first mom, another mom told me
the exact same story. She was really freaking out about this
just like I probably would have been, but when I told her
that I had heard the same exact thing no more than seven
days prior, she felt a sense of ease. She looked at me and
said, "Wait! It's not just my kid?" And when we're able to
say "It's not just my kid" in our own challenging moments,
we're able to approach our discipline and guidance with a
little bit more grace for both our children and ourselves.
That's why I'm honest with my mom friends. Whether
your child stole the five dollars you left on the counter or
they called your great-grandma "ugly" to her face, it can
be so helpful to have someone to unpack those things with
in an authentic, vulnerable way. I use both in-person and
online communities and forums where I can share honest
challenges. No, the opinions and experiences of other
parents obviously do not outweigh the advice of a trained
professional, and I'm aware that every child's development
is different, but these vulnerable conversations really help
remind me to approach my discipline in a much more
curious way.

3. **I ask the internet and I read books.** Now hear me out before you get all judgy! There actually is a really good amount of accurate digital and print information available. Of course, it requires some fact-checking and cross-referencing, but we literally Google everything else, so why not use the same resources to find parenting help? There's nothing wrong with Googling questions like "Is it typical for my child to tell me they hate me?" It is normal. With that said, it doesn't mean every parent hearing this should ignore the behavior. That's actually the opposite of intentional parenting. But they might approach the behavior with a little less angst. (Two of my favorite resources and mentors are Dr. Rebecca Kennedy, a clinical psychologist rightfully deemed "The Millennial Parenting Whisperer" by *Time* magazine, and Dr. Daniel Siegel, a clinical professor of psychiatry at the UCLA School of Medicine. I return to their teachings often in my parenting journey. And they have a pretty unfathomable amount of information on the internet. It's pretty incredible how much they share on this subject. I highly recommend checking out their digital and print resources!)

4. **I utilize a growth mindset.** The last and probably the most important thing I do when I'm trying to figure out what's going on with my kids is utilize a growth mindset. What my therapist says is great. What Google says is great… sometimes. What other parents in my community say is also great. But what matters most to me is what I'm actually seeing with my own eyes on a day-to-day basis. So many things can throw off "typical development," so I choose to look at my child where they are in the moment in comparison to where they've been to determine whether or not a behavior is appropriate for them. Trauma, major changes, and neurodiversity can all impact your child's behavior at any given point in their life. Our children are unique. Their experiences are unique. Maybe your child has experienced a divorce or the loss of a loved one, or has

gotten an ADHD diagnosis. All of those things probably are going to impact their development. Or maybe you just started intentional parenting and you've had years of unconscious parenting. That'll do it, too! So, while I do take outside support knowledge and resources very seriously, my biggest questions are these: Who is my child today in comparison to who they were yesterday? A month ago? Right after my divorce? That's what matters most to me. That's what allows me to look at my very vivacious four-year-old with grace when she has rare moments when she hits or kicks as opposed to two years ago when she was hitting every single day. Her brain is growing at her specific pace. And I can show up with my guidance based on who she is right now.

So here's the lesson: one of the most powerful things you can do as an intentional parent is to get curious about how to parent the child who's right in front of you!

What

In high school, my history teacher didn't use a calculator. Not even once. That's because it's not the most effective tool for teaching world history. He used maps, books, and videos, and I learned exactly what the class was designed to teach me—history. This illustrates the second of the three Ws: *what*. Before you can pick any specific tool, you have to actually know what it is that you're trying to teach your child and, conversely, what you're *not* trying to teach them.

When you're faced with the question "How do I respond to this behavior?" I'd like you to ask yourself this question: What am I trying to teach and what am I not trying to teach? This will help you pick discipline strategies that actually align with the lesson you're trying to help your child learn. When you don't ask this question, you run the risk of choosing a harmful strategy. And

8 Curiosity

choosing ineffective discipline can actually happen a lot easier than you think. Because many punitive forceful discipline techniques often change the behaviors, a parent might be led to believe the discipline is effective. For instance, picture a dad screaming at his son, telling him to apologize for hitting his little brother. While he may be teaching his child to apologize, he may not be conscious of the other messages he's sending. The child is also learning that it's okay to use force to get your way, just like the father did. That's pretty ironic considering that is exactly what the child was doing to get in trouble in the first place. This father is clearly choosing discipline that is not in alignment with his value of respecting others.

Let's look at some more examples of the contrast between what many parents are trying to teach versus what they are actually teaching.

Scenario

The child starts walking out of the house without hugging his grandpa.

What the parent wants to teach: The value of warmth and connection toward loved ones.

The parent's response: "Stop acting like that. Go give Grandpa a hug."

What the parent may also be teaching the child: Your physical boundaries don't matter.

Scenario

The child won't stop screaming and jumping on the couch.

What the parent wants to teach: How to respect other people's things.

The parent's response: "You're misbehaving. Go to time-out."

What the parent may also be teaching the child: When you're overstimulated, I won't support you.

Scenario

The child forgot to do the dishes but the parent just ignored the behavior. They forgot to wash the dishes again the next day.

What the parent wants to teach: Responsibility.

The parent's response: "Give me your phone."

What the parent may also be teaching the child: You can't trust your environment because I give out unpredictable mood-based, fear-based, or ego-based punishments.

In each of these scenarios, the parent has a pretty reasonable lesson they're trying to teach the child, but they're not conscious of the other unintended lessons they're teaching the child as well. If you're not careful, you can teach your children lessons that go against your core values. So before you choose how you're going to discipline, ask yourself what else you might be teaching your child with this strategy. Consider whether it is in alignment with, or in contrast to, your personal values as an intentional parent. These scenarios might seem a bit obvious, but there will always be numerous opportunities to ask yourself the question "What else did I just teach my child?"

You can teach your child how to show affection, respect, kindness, and so many other things without compromising your values. So before you choose how to respond to your child's behavior, make sure you have a clear strategy on what you are trying to teach them and what you are *not trying* to teach them. This will make it a whole lot easier to determine what feels right for you and what will be most effective for your child. And if you value connection, forced, isolating time-outs just don't

8 Curiosity

make sense. If you value respect, spanking just doesn't make sense. If you value communication, yelling just doesn't make sense.

I can recall a time where I asked my daughter not to run in the kitchen because I spilled water. When she did it anyway and slipped and fell, I asked her if she was okay. But can you guess what came out of my mouth immediately after that? "See, I told you that would happen." I know I'm not the first to use this seemingly harmless phrase. Parents often use "I told you so" as a way of reiterating a lesson, but this phrase can also send some harmful messages. The point is that you can teach your child how to show affection, respect, kindness, and so many other things without compromising your values.

"I told you it was cold outside. Put your jacket on."

"I told you your brother would get mad. Don't go in his room."

"I told you you'd spill the ice cream cone. You should have gotten a cup."

I used to do it all the time. It was like saying, "See? I was right. You can trust me. I know what I'm talking about." But when I asked myself if there was anything else that I was teaching my daughter with this phrase, I realized a lot more came with it.

"I was right. But also, you were wrong."

"You can trust me. But also, you can't trust yourself to make decisions."

"I know what I'm talking about, you don't."

That epiphany hit me like a ton of bricks. Personal power is literally one of my values, but there I was, taking my child's personal power away from her. We all have those moments when we realize our parenting isn't in alignment with our values. And I'm sure I'll have more of those moments. But it's my curiosity and asking yourself the questions "What am I trying to teach?" and "What am

I not trying to teach?" that allows me to get back in harmony with what matters to me as an intentional parent.

When

The last W of curiosity is *when*. Before you discipline your child, consider the question of *when* is the most appropriate time to help your child with a behavior. As I mentioned earlier, many of us have been practicing reactive parenting, which means that when we overpersonalize our children's behaviors, there's a strong sense of urgency to fix them. But "immediately" is more often than not the worst time to support our children in learning new behaviors.

If you're shocked to hear that discipline actually doesn't need to happen immediately following a behavior, you're not alone. The idea of pausing before reacting is counter to what a lot of us learned as we were growing up. It boils my blood to think how much literature there is instructing parents to give out consequences to children as quickly as possible to ensure that they understand the connection between their behavior and the parent's response. But this is not logical, flexible, or even necessary. In fact, it can actually be counterproductive. This urgent desire to fix a child's behavior doesn't take into account their developmental stage, and it certainly doesn't take into account the parent's values. Let's just throw that nonsense out the window right now! In order to figure out a more appropriate time to discipline, consider your family's rhythms.

Rhythms are the fluctuations you see in your moods, energy, and receptivity. Sometimes our rhythms are thrown off by major life events. When you are curious during these periods, you can make more informed decisions. When we moved, I knew my daughter was facing a lot of change. I recognized that her rhythms were completely thrown off, so I was able to help her slowly transition. Had I not been curious, I likely would have been far more on edge about the behaviors that resulted from the move and far less available to support her through the transition. Of course, your children aren't always going through major life changes, so they probably have at least a few predictable rhythms that can help you determine the most effective time and way to discipline. The same is true for you. There are moments when you are more able to give positive, compassionate support and discipline. Intentional parents are curious about understanding these predictable family rhythms and adapting to when rhythms are thrown off so they can determine the most effective time and way to discipline. Again, it's not about any one particular discipline strategy. Rather, it's about being open and curious so you can find what's best for the moment, choosing what's most effective for your family based on the principle of curiosity.

Let's consider how to better understand your family's rhythms and how they can help you determine and create the best tools for your family.

Your Child's Moods

We'll start with understanding your child's *moods*. Your child experiences stressors every single day. They also have very unique brains growing inside their head. So, of course, you're not going to be able to predict their moods one hundred percent of the time, but that doesn't mean that there aren't some patterns. You know your kid. You know when they're more anxious, more angry, more sensitive, more irritable. You also know when they're more happy, excited, and joyful. If you're unsure, spend a couple of weeks tracking their daily behaviors to see if you notice any patterns. Pay attention to your child's mood in the mornings, when they're playing, after school, during dinner time, and before bedtime. By getting curious, you're more likely to start seeing some consistencies. It's also important to pay attention to the peaks and valleys of your mood.

For example, let's say teeth brushing is a pretty big challenge in your house before bedtime. If your child is giving you a hard time about this, consider your child's rhythms. If they are typically dysregulated right after dinner, that's also not a good time to go right into the teeth brushing routine. Instead, you might want to support your child in regulating before you even head to the bathroom. It's really compassionate and considerate to wait until they are regulated, calm, and operating with more logic and less emotion before you face a challenge together.

You'll also want to consider whether you are feeling triggered. Maybe you just scrolled social media for an hour and now you're feeling exceptionally bad about yourself like you always do after a social media binge. If you are, that's not a good teaching moment, and if you proceed with an immediate response, you're probably going to lean into the situation with force or fear. Maybe, instead, you put the toothbrush down, go call your best friend for a good laugh, and try again in a few minutes.

That doesn't have to mean you'll always have to step away for thirty minutes and go phone a friend. You may not have the flexibility to do that in every situation. But, can you at least try to pause, name your feelings, take a deep breath, and slow your heart rate a bit before you choose a strategy to encourage your child to brush their teeth? Absolutely! This is especially true if you are creating more safety for your nervous system as we previously discussed.

I don't know about you, but this approach was pretty scary for me at first. If the thought of not reacting also freaks you out a bit, that's okay. But if you keep running into moments where you feel like crap because of the discipline strategy you've chosen, then you have to allow yourself to choose a time where you and your child are operating in the social engagement (ventral vagal) state. This will enable you to teach with logic and compassion, and your child can then receive it with logic and compassion. So even when your child is throwing a tantrum around that judgmental relative, just pause. As a matter of fact, *especially* when your child is throwing a tantrum around that judgmental relative, just pause and lean into a quick calming tool. The more intense your emotions are in a given situation, the less you should be doing to teach, fix, or correct in that moment. All you need to do is create a safe space for yourself and your child and then allow yourselves to more slowly move through the moment.

Your Child's Energy

The next thing to consider is your child's *energy*. This is especially true for more serious discipline moments. If you need to have a more intense conversation with your child, you may want to consider if they are tired, overstimulated, or hyperfocusing their energy on a specific task or activity. If so, you may want to address their energy before disciplining or choose a strategy that is better suited for the moment and then circle back for that deeper conversation. Maybe you help them regulate their energy before you have that conversation. Maybe you both come up with a reasonable time to discuss the topic rather than forcing them to stop right that second. Maybe you talk after they take a nap.

For example, my youngest is calm and energized every morning. But my oldest? Not so much. It's the complete opposite scenario with our nighttime routine. My nine-year-old is much more vibrant in the evenings than my four-year-old. Once I recognized these patterns, it was pretty simple to determine how to show up for my children. In the mornings, when my nine-year-old was talking back or moving slowly, I would still step in and help her, but I would discipline her with the understanding that she's just more moody in the mornings. I wouldn't lecture her or use long-form discipline. Instead, I would opt for quicker, more empathetic ways of helping her with her behavior. Things like redirection (which will be discussed later) were more suited for these moments. The same goes for our evenings with the four-year-old. I would approach the evenings as gently as possible. I would reserve the mornings to be a bit more intense with applying my guidance and tools.

Some discipline strategies just do not work well when our children are overstimulated or when they're putting their energy into something they really enjoy or when they're just plain old tired. A child playing at the park may not be able to leave when you're using strategies like rationalization to convince them it's time to go. In this case, playfully transitioning to the car ("Let's bounce like bunnies all the way to the car!") might be a useful strategy. Likewise, you'll likely need a different approach to convince a teenager to take out the trash when they are devoting all their energy to the video game versus when they are not. It's understandable if the teenager has a difficult time complying with the request the first time around. Still, the trash needs to go out; you value cleanliness and you want to be consistent with teaching them responsibility. So, you choose a strategy that still acknowledges how hard it is to stop playing the video game. That may mean you both agree that she'll take the trash out after she's done playing the video game. That may mean you set a timer for ten minutes, at which point she'll take a break and take the trash out. That may mean you sit down and play with her and take over to slay the dragon after five minutes so she can go take the trash out. Even as adults, we find it hard to shift our energy from one thing to the next. This is especially true when we're shifting from a desirable activity to one we don't enjoy. There are so many workable options in these scenarios, but the important point is that you're actually considering your child's stimulation level before you're choosing your response.

It's important to ask yourself if you have the capacity to lean into your child's rhythms and choose a strategy that honors the child that is showing up right in front of you, as opposed to the child you *want* to be showing up in front of you. When your child is overstimulated, what works? What helps you move through the moment? What doesn't work? What amplifies a power struggle? When is your child tired? How can you help rather than force them through these moments? Understanding the rhythm of your child's energy will help you better lean more fully into what's working at any given time or to stop, reset, and try something different.

8   Curiosity

Your Child's Receptivity

Lastly, let's talk about *receptivity*. A pretty profound question you can ask yourself is when is your child most receptive to these lessons. I say this all the time: most things are not emergencies. If you're trying to teach your three-year-old to stop blowing spit bubbles, that is not an emergency. This means that if a strategy is not working, it's no big deal to shift and try something else. It also means that it's actually okay if you have to take a step back because you have no clue what to do right in that moment. The same is true for a teen having a meltdown. Maybe you try rationalization because that usually works, but for some reason today it's making things worse. If you're conscious of your child's receptivity, you can back off that strategy and try another. Once you've successfully moved through the moment, you can analyze it with curiosity. What was different? Maybe your child's less receptive when their friends are around. Maybe they're less receptive when you're on your phone.

Every child is different, but they do leave us clues about their receptivity. Sometimes it's more obvious than others, but when we are curious, we are much more likely to understand what will and won't be appropriate for a given situation. I love to teach my children my values by sharing stories from my past that relate to their experiences. But through practicing curiosity, I've noticed that my oldest daughter isn't very receptive to my little childhood anecdotes in the moments she's telling me about her own experiences. Storytelling has been a very effective tool for us. However, I now use it with caution to ensure that it is well-received (remember, I desire to be understood, not just heard). I've realized I probably shouldn't share personal stories when she's sharing all the social drama from her day when we're on the way home from school. Instead, I choose to use it in absolutely random moments when we're not talking about her experiences. I'll still think of a lesson while she's sharing, but I hold my tongue. Later on, while we're cooking together (connecting), I might say, "Hey, I just thought about something that happened when I was seven years old. Can I share it?" I still get to use the story to teach whatever lesson I'm trying to teach, but I choose to do so when my child is actually receptive. Sometimes the tool is not the issue. Sometimes it's about finding the most appropriate time to use that tool so that it is received in the way you intended it. Here are some journal prompts to help you with curiosity:

- What behaviors are your children exhibiting that are a challenge for you?

- Based on your child's individual pace, are these behaviors developmentally appropriate?

- If not, what resources can you look into to better support your child?

- Think of the last time you used some form of discipline. What were you trying to teach? Can you think of any other messages you may have also sent?

- Is your child currently facing any major life changes that might make discipline a bit more challenging?

- Has your child experienced any traumas, major changes, or developmental challenges that are impacting them currently?

- When is your child most receptive to learning from you?

- When is your child more distant, shut down, overstimulated, combative, or unfocused?

9

Collaboration
(Defining Roles and Working Together)

Say this to yourself: "My child really wants to cooperate with me!"

If that felt awkward or a little untrue, it's probably because quite often you've experience the opposite. You may be thinking, "My child wants the opposite of cooperation. My child is intentionally pushing the limits and working against me for sport. If they wanted to cooperate, they wouldn't take ten minutes to put their shoes on!" If that rings true, it may not feel like your child wants to be on the same page with you. Yes, they may challenge your limits at different stages in their development, but what is also true is that many of us—me included—have spent a lot of time using parenting tools that work *against* a collaborative environment, and that may be contributing to how your child responds. You may find yourself constantly yelling, punishing, and bribing because your children just don't listen. But I want to offer you a fresh perspective. What if your children aren't listening *because* of the yelling, punishing, and bribing? If we condition our children to only cooperate when we flex our authority, they have no reason to do so when we don't. And that just means more yelling, punishing, and bribing in the future.

What if there's another way? What if your child actually *does* want to work with you? What if they would love to feel like an active participant in the culture of your home? What if they actually want to be on the same team? It's possible. But it means you have to start treating them more like a teammate. It requires you to move away from the idea that you are the almighty authority handing out rules and regulations. Think about it: if it's only your house and your rules, then your child only has one reason to respect those rules, and that's fear. Either they fear a negative consequence (*my mom will yell if I do this*) or they fear losing a positive reward (*I won't get to play on my computer if I do that*). The problem with this approach is that they may struggle to follow the rules when there's no real consequence. They'll associate the behavior with the positive or negative consequences but won't build an intrinsic motivation for those behaviors. So when the praise or punishment isn't present, the behavior may not persist. Put plainly, they won't respond until you yell or offer them the candy! When we use a "because I said so" parenting style, we completely miss the opportunity to give them a sense of responsibility over their actions. Simply put, we compromise on teaching our kids integrity for the sake of compliance. I want my children to make good decisions with or without the fear of a punishment or the promise of a reward. And that means I have to be intentional about creating an environment where they have a sense of ownership over their actions. I have to prioritize the third "C" of Intentional Parenting: *collaboration*.

Creating a Collaborative Environment in Your Home

As intentional parents, we are committed to the belief that our children deserve love, kindness, and respect. As a result, we are far more aware when fairness and empathy are not present in our parenting styles. Most parents would never say that their children don't deserve fairness and empathy, but their actions would suggest

9 Collaboration

otherwise. Intentional parents work to align their actions with their words. We have to walk the walk and exemplify the belief that our children are born worthy of our respect. And because we understand our children's innate value, it just makes sense that we also value their input and collaborate with them to create the family culture. We aren't the big wise sages we think we are. Our children actually have a lot to offer and teach us if we are open to it. And collaboration allows us to show our children we are open to, and grateful for, who they are. It's the only way to honor everyone in the family. When you parent without collaboration, someone loses. Either you move into permissive parenting and place too much emphasis on the child's input or you move into authoritarian parenting and put too much emphasis on your own input. But the cool thing about intentional parenting is that everyone wins. Now don't get me wrong. There will definitely be moments where you are making a greater sacrifice. There will also be moments where your child doesn't get their way. Both your input and effort, and your child's input and effort, will vary at different stages in your journey. Collaboration when your child is a one-year-old will look very different than when your child is sixteen. But the overall culture of your home will be rooted in teamwork and equity.

There's an analogy that is often used in authoritarian parenting and it's that the family is a corporation. It's typically used to describe the hierarchy of the family: the parents are usually the owners or bosses, while the children are employees. And I think it's a terrible use of such a potentially amazing analogy. The idea that a family is a corporation really has potential, especially in regard to collaboration. Unfortunately, it just falls short of describing a corporation that I'd be proud to work for. In other words, I'd hate to be a part of *that* family. So I'm going to flip the analogy on its head. The kind of corporation I'd like to be a part of has a lot more fluidity in its hierarchy. This kind of corporation is collaborative and values the input of everyone involved. And so I'm going to break down the principle of collaboration with a much more intentional use of this analogy. We'll explore two key elements of the kind of company I'd like to be a part of—a solid mission statement and clear roles and expectations.

Let's do it!

Create a Family Mission Statement

A few years ago I was on a work trip and my boss told me we would be staying at someone's house. Now, I'm not the most picky person in the world, but I wasn't thrilled to be sleeping in a stranger's home. And I wasn't just being difficult, but it really didn't make sense. I was working for a huge company at the time, so I was a bit confused as to why this billion-dollar business had eight of us staying at somebody's house instead of at a hotel. I was low-key offended, to be honest. And to add insult to injury, they had the nerve to wait until we got all the way to Georgia to tell us this? The audacity! I could have stayed at home!

But the people pleaser in me dared not complain. So I forced myself not to roll my eyes as we passed by several perfectly suitable hotels to get to where we were staying. When we finally arrived, all I could do was laugh at myself for wanting to stay at a hotel and for doing that thing again where I jump the gun with assumptions. We pulled up to an incredible mansion equipped with an elevator, a gym, and multiple kitchens. I didn't even know that was a thing. The house was amazing! It was so big, in fact, that I legitimately got lost several times while I was there. It was like its own little city. Every inch of the house was breathtaking and so well kept; it put the best hotel in the area to shame. But this is not what left me in awe. Even more amazing than the house was the experience. When I walked into the bedroom I was staying in (which, by the way, had its own freaking kitchen), I instantly felt like it was my home. The room had my favorite snacks, some personal items, and even a handwritten note for me. As I sat on my bed, reading my note and eating my Pringles, the very first word that came to my mind was *hospitality*.

9 Collaboration

That night the experience went from great to phenomenal. The hosts prepared a meal for the team and sat down and ate with us. I don't remember what we ate, but I do remember being brought seconds! Yes, I said "brought" because we didn't make our plates. At that moment, another word came to mind: *service*. In addition to the amazing meal, they also had the most lovely family and we shared some of the warmest conversations I've ever had. During dinner I realized that their children had all given up their rooms for us and that they would also be having dinner with us every night of our stay. I had never met a more hospitable and serving family in my life. But here's what really blew my mind: I learned that this was what they did. Like, this was their *thing*. They invited people in need of a short stay into their home and treated them like family. All night long they shared stories of people in transitions and groups on mission trips that they had hosted. And their children were enthused about the experience. They were just as passionate about the dynamic as their parents. And it didn't feel forced at all. The kids were genuinely excited about their involvement. I was confused! How many children do you know that are thrilled to give up their rooms or regularly have dinner with complete strangers? This was not by accident. There was some intentional parenting going on here.

Now, the chain of events that led them to this lifestyle isn't what's relevant here. And to be quite honest, my ADHD won't let me remember them anyway! What I want to share with you is the part that I have held on to for all of these years. I had to ask what inspired them to start doing this and how they kept all of it up. Somewhere in the conversation the father held his wife's hand and said, "When we realized this is what we wanted to do, we sat down and wrote out a vision for our family. We also have a mission statement that embodies what we stand for as a family." I asked, "A family what? A mission who?" And I instantly clung to that and wanted to hear more. As they kept talking, I wasn't surprised to realize that the common themes were—you guessed it—hospitality and service. Literally the words I had been using to describe this family all day were exactly what they were striving for. This was the first moment I experienced the power of a mission statement. Unfortunately, it wasn't until years later that I implemented the collaborative practice of creating a mission statement, and I honestly wish it had been sooner. It's just one of those things that instantly changes the vibe in a family. This is especially true if you've been using disempowering forms of discipline. When done with compassion, curiosity, and effective communication, creating a family mission statement can instantly empower your children.

So it's time to create your own vision and mission statement for your company... I mean, your family! Keep in mind that this may not all happen in one sitting and will likely be an ongoing process that you revisit as a family. Here's how you do it.

Step 1: Find a Time That Works For Everyone to Discuss the Family's Vision

In the first section of this book, you discovered your core values. Now it's time to help your child find theirs! Explain to your child that you all are going to be coming up with a family mission statement. A less formal description may work for some children. You can call it a family "motto," family "values," family "rules," or anything else that might work. It should be something that resonates with you *and* your children. During this meeting, you are going to get curious about your children's values. You've already taken time to figure out what matters to you so that you can be an intentional parent, and now it's time to figure out what matters to your children so you can become an intentional family.

Using the same list of value questions from chapter 1, it's time to explore your child's values. The answers to the following questions will better help you understand your child's values. Remember: our children communicate in their own special ways. Whether your child is younger, is nonverbal, or just has a hard time articulating their feelings, you can meet them where they are developmentally and tailor this practice to suit them. For some families, that may mean asking specific questions. For others, you may need to use pictures, songs, or games, while some families will have to pay attention to their child's behaviors and preferences over time to get an understanding of their values. There's no one-size-fits-all way to do this. What matters most is that you're including your child's input in whatever way they are able to give it.

Questions for discovering your child's values:

- What kinds of things make you smile?
- What kinds of things make you feel frustrated?
- What do you love that I do?
- What do you wish I did differently?
- What's your favorite thing about yourself?
- If you could do one thing all day, what would it be?
- When do you feel safe?
- Do you ever feel embarrassed? When?
- What makes you feel special?
- What are you good at?
- What do you wish you were better at?
- What am I good at?
- Who are your heroes? Who do you admire? What do they do that you find admirable?
- How do you think other people should be treated?
- How do you think you should be treated?
- What are five things that are really important to you?
- What do you like to do with us?
- What do you like to do by yourself?
- What is something that you absolutely cannot stand?
- What makes you feel nervous?

- Name a time when you felt super excited!
- When do you feel calm or peaceful?
- If you could change one thing about the world, what would it be?

Finish by asking them to complete this statement: "I love _____."

If your child is open to it and if you can follow up any of these questions with "why?" you'll be able to get an even deeper understanding of their values. Once you've explored these topics (and hopefully added some of your own) you should have a better understanding of what matters to your child.

At this point, you can sift through the answers to find your child's values. If they're willing, have them go through the values list and then choose three to five that *really* resonate with them. If they're not willing to take this extra step, this exercise is going to require just a little bit more curiosity on your end. Every answer that you get from your child will have clues as to what is important to them. For example, if your child says "I love reading" and "I wish I was better at math," your child may value knowledge or academics. If you notice that your child is at peace when they're coloring or excited when playing with Legos, they may value creativity or innovation. If your child says they're good at making friends and admire the popular girl on their favorite TV show, then they may value social status.

At this point, you may not be on the same page with your child, and this could bring up some real triggers for you. That's okay! My oldest really values social status right now. I love her for who she is. And the more I'm able to accept what is important to her, the more open she'll be to adopting some of my values. Remember, this is not about right and wrong, so it's not our job to change our children's values. The family mission statement will incorporate *everybody's* values. So once they share their values, simply thank them and take some time to share yours. I'd imagine that some of your values won't be at the top of your children's lists, so it's okay if some of theirs don't resonate with you, either. Collaboration is about taking in both what matters to them and what matters to you. Everyone's needs and desires deserve a space in the company culture!

Step 2: Create Your Family's List of Core Values

Now it's time to narrow down the list. How you do that is up to you. Whether you have a long list or a short list, you need to make sure the list isn't dominated by the values of the parent or the child. Maybe you can all rank your values and then take the top three from everyone. Or maybe your list will consist mostly of shared values and will incorporate a few individual values from each family member. There's really only one rule: keep it collaborative and fair.

Step 3: Organize Your Family's Values into a Mission Statement

This may mean that everyone gets to come up with a sentence to describe the mission statement or that your children serve as editors for the sentences that you come up with. (Your little ones might like to write it out on a piece of paper and decorate it.) Just make sure that everyone has an opportunity to contribute. How you draft your family mission statement is also up to you. Maybe you use complete sentences or maybe you'll use bullet points. Just try not to make it too long; you'll want to keep it short to make revisiting it easy. There will be moments when you will all need reminders of what's important to you, so let's not make it a long-winded reminder! If it takes longer than one minute to recite your mission statement, it's too long! This is especially true if you have smaller children in your house. When my kids were younger, our mission statement embodied all of our values, but it was only three words: *fun, love,* and *pixie dust.* Mashed into that tiny little slogan was the importance of creativity, adventure, compassion, kindness, passion, play, and so many other things that are important to us.

Here are a few examples to help you get started:

Our family mission: We find fun and adventure as often as possible. We treat others with kindness, and respect one another. We celebrate each other's gifts and differences and get through challenges together. We give each other patience, support, and love.

or

In our house:

- We keep our arms, ears, and hearts open.
- We work hard and play harder.
- We believe anything is possible.
- We give more than we receive.
- We say "yes" to fun.
- We take care of each other.
- We put love first.

or

As a family:

- We do hard things.
- We are creators.
- We love big.
- We are kind, caring, and compassionate.
- We are learners, and are not afraid of failure.
- We have fun and laugh often.
- We believe in ourselves.
- We treat ourselves, our community, and our world with respect.

9 Collaboration

Step 4: Display Your Mission Statement in a Prominent Place

This visual reminder will be helpful for both you and your children. You'll be able to see it every day and remember everyone's values. At times when you need a more powerful reminder, you can read it aloud to your children. However, you'll want to avoid using the mission statement coercively or for negative reinforcement. For example, if your child is hitting, I wouldn't recommend bringing them to your framed mission statement. You want your child to feel a sense of ownership over the mission statement, and if you use it punitively it will likely feel more like yours than theirs. Or worse, it can induce shame, like in moments when your child is struggling to embody the mission. Shame is not the best foundation for transformation. It can weaken a child's desire for collaboration and make cultivating your family's values much more difficult. Instead, I like to use the mission statement preventatively. If your children go to your co-parent's house, you may want to make going over the mission statement a fun reintroduction back into their environment with you. Maybe you incorporate the mission statement into your daily routine by reciting it when you pick them up from school. Try to visit the mission statement as often as possible without making it a negative experience for your child. Stay true to the principle of collaboration when considering when and how you revisit your mission statement.

It's also important to revise your mission statement when necessary. As an adult, you may be a bit more rooted in your values and they may not change all that significantly over time. But this is often not the case for our children. As they grow and learn who they are, their values will likely change, so you'll want to make room for their expansion. Getting to know your child is a continuous process. Show them that they matter throughout that process by revising the mission statement to meet their present needs and values as time goes on.

It is my hope that just by taking this first step, your child will see how important who they are is to you. If you've never done something like this before, you may be shocked at how quickly something so simple can expand the connection and intimacy in your home. It's a wonderful practice and I return to it as my children continue to grow, develop, and become who they are.

Create Clear Roles and Expectations

Every good company has clearly defined roles and responsibilities. How else would the individuals contribute to the company's mission? And how are you and your family going to make sure your family vision is carried out? Well, you're going to do it as a team, of course. You're going to collaborate! More specifically, everyone's going to have a role to play. Both you and your children have responsibilities in the family. And everyone needs to know what defines success in their position. That's why these roles and expectations need to be as clear as possible. Think about it. If you worked for a company and you had no clue what you were supposed to do, it would be really difficult to feel secure in your position. How would you know when you're getting it right? How would you know when you're getting it wrong? If you don't have a clear job description, you have no clue how to effectively contribute to the team. Without clarity, you're left to figure it out on your own. You wouldn't think the company valued your position. And that's just no fun!

The same is true for your children. They want to contribute. We are innately communal, so they want to collaborate with you, but that's really difficult to do when expectations are unclear or constantly changing. So it's time to shift into even more intentionality and define your child's role in the process, as well as your own role in the process.

Defining Your Roles

There are some specific roles you will play as an intentional parent. Think of yourself as "The Chief Safety Officer," "The Chief Love

9   Collaboration

Officer," and "The Chief Guidance Officer." It's your job to keep them safe, love them, and guide them. Our children are new to the company. They're fresh out of "college" and have very little experience! And it is our job to train them to eventually become the "officers" in their own lives. Eventually, we want our children to be able to love themselves and others. We want them to be able to have their own internal guidance system. And we want them to know how to respect both their own boundaries as well as the boundaries of others. When it comes to discipline, collaboration is about staying in our role and allowing our children to be introduced to, learn, adapt to, and eventually master certain responsibilities at a realistic pace.

Dr. Becky, who I mentioned earlier, is also a fan of this analogy, and she put it this way: "You wouldn't just hand over all of your responsibilities to an intern." Similarly, it isn't logical to think that our children should be able to handle the roles in our department. At least, not yet! That means we uphold the boundaries, we model love, and we support them in making appropriate decisions. Let's look at these three roles individually.

Chief Safety Officer

We have to keep these little people alive. We have to make sure their environments are safe and that they interact safely with others. It's a tough job! That's why we need boundaries. Remember, the boundary is the moat that guards the castle. It's not your job to force your children to behave. It's your job to create boundaries that support your children's behavior. It's not your child's responsibility to know how to regulate their emotions at age three, so not hitting someone might be above their competency level. But what if one of your family values is respecting others' physical space? Do you just let your son lay the smackdown on his sister? No! You're the "Chief Safety Officer." So what makes sense for that role? Well, you're not going to just sit there and keep asking him to stop. That doesn't keep the other child safe. And you're not going to yell at him because that infringes on his safety. You're going to step in with a boundary. You need a barrier! You need to clearly define what you are willing to allow in the moment. That could look like holding his hand or removing him from the room until he's regulated. The point is, you set the boundary.

(When we don't set boundaries, we become permissive.)

Chief Love Officer

But what happens when your kids freak out? Maybe they don't like that they have to stop playing, so they start sobbing uncontrollably. What do you do then? That's when you step in as the "Chief Love Officer." It's time to validate some feelings! It's time to hold space for their emotions. It's time to support them as they operate in the emotional part of their brain. It's not your job to force them back into rationalization. It's not your responsibility to fix their feelings. (Those feelings will exist whether we acknowledge them or not.) The only way for them to move through those feelings is with our support by accepting their feelings and allowing them to express them. But what's most important is to regulate yourself, acknowledge their emotions, and support them as they slowly move back up the emotional ladder and into the ventral vagal state.

(When we don't give them empathy, we become authoritarian.)

Chief Guidance Officer

Okay, so you didn't just let your kid hit their sibling. You stopped the action by holding their hands or taking them to a quiet corner and practicing empathy. You gave them an opportunity to cry, express their frustration, and show you they were upset about your boundary. Once everyone is regulated and feeling safe, you get to do what most people think is the main job of a parent—tell them what to do. And by that I just mean you get to use a discipline strategy to guide them toward more appropriate behavior. (We'll discuss some strategies for this in the next chapter). Even as gentle parents, we do not just throw the lesson away.

9 Collaboration

(When we don't guide our children, we become passive.)

So you're "The Chief Safety Officer," "The Chief Love Officer," and "The Chief Guidance Officer." When you're deciding on an appropriate discipline strategy, make sure you don't choose something that conflicts with your roles! Ask yourself:

"Will this make my child less safe?"

"Will this require me to lose empathy for my child?"

"Will this decision keep me from helping my child learn this skill?"

The more you lean into these three roles in your parenting, the easier it will be to cultivate secure attachments with your child.

Your Child's Role

So what's your child's role in collaboration? Well, eventually they're going to take your job, but right now, they're just newbies. They're interns! They're here to soak up the culture and give you a ton of opportunities to train them in your role. That's why I like to call children "Chief Authenticity Officers." We create a safe space for them and they get to show us who they are. They get to feel and be themselves. In fact, in order for us to do our jobs, we need them to do just that! The moments when they aren't listening are our opportunities to teach them boundaries. The moments when they are throwing tantrums are our opportunities to teach them compassion and regulation. And the moments where they're behaving inappropriately are our opportunities to guide them toward new behaviors. Lucky for us, they're really good at the role of "Chief Authenticity Officer" from the moment they open their eyes. They know how to be themselves until they're coerced to do otherwise. It's your child's job to call you the "worst parent ever." And it's your job to keep their feelings safe by validating their experience with words like, "You're allowed to be angry at me." It's your responsibility to model compassion so they can eventually learn how to give it. And it's your responsibility to teach them a more appropriate way to express their anger.

Believe it or not, when your child is about to hurl that toy at their friend while they're on a playdate, that's a part of their job, too. You're not afraid of the behavior because you know it's age appropriate and you're ready to step into your role. So you keep the other child safe by grabbing the toy and then you model empathy with words like "You must be having a really tough time right now." And then you guide them both toward more appropriate, safer play.

I'm not surprised if it's a little unsettling for you to think that it's actually your child's job to show you inappropriate behaviors. It's a really inconvenient set-up, isn't it? Am I really telling you that your child is *supposed* to hate mornings, call their sister dumb, rip up an important document, lie, and so on? I kind of am. It's not their job to know what to do all the time. So they are going to mess up and make their own unique mistakes. If you accept this as a part of *their* job, it'll be a lot easier to lean into *your* job! Take a breath. Do not panic, because you *still* can have expectations of them. Remember, they need responsibilities, too. How can they collaborate with you and work as a team if you don't expect them to do anything? That's setting them up for failure. And it's honestly where a lot of people get confused about conscious parenting. They think that just because we give our children grace and understanding that we don't have any expectations of them. That's not the case. You are an intentional parent, not a passive parent, so you do need to outline expectations. Otherwise, the "company" can't thrive!

Having Clear Expectations

Everyone on the team has needs and desires. Your needs are not more important than your child's and vice versa. We make sure everyone's needs are met by working together and meeting clear expectations. This is the heart of collaboration and it's especially important to remember this during challenging moments. If you're struggling with mornings, you all need clear responsibilities that are

9 Collaboration

in alignment with your roles. The same goes for other challenges. Nighttime routines, eating, homework, room cleaning, running errands—think about the moments that are a bit more challenging for your family. Those moments are where it's easy for one person's needs to go unmet if you're not intentional. These are the moments that need clear expectations. This will allow you to be proactive in your parenting and set your children up for success in their roles.

For example, grocery shopping with a child can be a nightmare for some. It's the parent's job to set up clear grocery store expectations for the child based on the challenges they typically face. Here are some possible pre-grocery store conversations:

"Hey, we're about to go to the grocery store. It's your job to have fun. So you can sing and play and laugh all you want. It's my job to keep you safe. So I'm not willing to let you do anything dangerous. I expect you to walk and stay close to me while you play. And if you have a hard time with that, I will help you by putting you in the basket. Let's go have some fun."

or

"We are about to go to the grocery store and you're going to see a lot of things that you want. I expect you to want those things. I'm not willing to buy any candy today. I will buy you a snack. You get to pick out your snack! If you have a hard time with this decision, I will step in and help you."

or

"We're about to go into the grocery store. I know you hate stores. I don't expect you to want to go. I do expect you to use your kind words and make requests rather than demands if you get frustrated."

The expectations will depend on your child's developmental stage and your family's personal values. Whatever they are, it's helpful to express them prior to the challenging moment and as clearly as possible. This will increase the likelihood of a less challenging moment. Keep in mind though that even when we set expectations, they shouldn't be rigid. We're allowed to change course. Flexibility is not permissive. There will be moments where changing an expectation doesn't compromise your values. If you get to the grocery store and remember that the kids are off from school the next day, maybe you'll have the capacity for buying that candy because an evening sugar rush won't be detrimental to their routines the next morning. Maybe you see how desperately your child needs physical activity, so instead of resisting it and expecting them to walk, you lean into it and invite them to hop like a bunny.

My Only Nonnegotiable: Safety

Most of our expectations will have some degree of flexibility. They have to if we want to practice collaborative discipline. Everyone's needs can't be prioritized when there's too much rigidity. This is not to say that everything should be flexible, though. There are going to be some nonnegotiable expectations. For me and many parents in my community, those nonnegotiables are safety-related. While I'm flexible with most things, I have very little flexibility when it comes to safety. For example, I teach my children to use their manners. However, there's some flexibility there. While I encourage my children to say "thank you" and "excuse me," I never force them to do so and I can adjust this expectation when appropriate. Safety, however, is a totally different ball game. Whether they want to or not, they have to wear a seat belt, stay out of the middle of the street, and stay off the coffee table! I create firmer boundaries around these things. You'll want to clarify your nonnegotiable expectations for your children and remind them that it is your responsibility to keep them safe. Of course, you will do your very best to honor your children's values while keeping them safe, and you'll do that as often as you can; however, you want to let them know that their safety outweighs everything else.

One day my daughter and I were walking on a path in the woods near our house when she bent down to pick up a leaf. Now, I'm

9 Collaboration

no botanist, but any time I see little white beads growing with the leaves, I assume it's poison ivy. The leaf she was about to pick up definitely had poison ivy vibes, so I quickly snatched her up and moved her away from the plant. She immediately started sobbing. "You grabbed me! You grabbed me!" We both really valued personal physical space and we talked about this often, so she felt like I completely ignored that value. And she was absolutely right—I did! So I apologized to her, validated her feelings, and helped her calm down. Once she was calm, I asked her if she was open to me explaining why I picked her up so quickly. I explained to her what poison ivy was and I even showed her a picture. I told her that next time she might be able to spot the poison ivy herself, and if she did she should try very hard not to touch it. I reminded her that it was my job to keep her safe and that I would do that no matter what, even if that meant picking her up without asking. And then I reassured her that I would only do that if it was a matter of safety. I began using the language of "nonnegotiables" at a very young age and now that she's nine years old, she knows exactly what that means and can differentiate between negotiable and nonnegotiable safety expectations.

And that's the wonderful thing about a collaborative environment. Our children really do become more collaborative over time. They are able to take on more roles and responsibilities as they grow. When we are making value-based decisions, staying true to our missions, operating in our roles, and working with clear expectations, our families have a much better chance to thrive! Here are some journal prompts for collaboration:

- Do you think your family would be comfortable coming up with a mission statement? If not, how can you make this process more suitable for your family dynamic?
- How do you show up in your role as "Chief Safety Officer"?
- How do you show up in your role as "Chief Love Officer"?

- How do you show up in your role as "Chief Guidance Officer"?

- How comfortable are you with letting your child make mistakes and be "Chief Authenticity Officer"?

- How comfortable are you with expressing expectations proactively rather than expressing them reactively?

- What are your nonnegotiables?

10

Communication
(Having Empowering Conversations)

We have to dismantle the idea that we are all-knowing and smarter than our children, and that they desperately need our guidance in order to become good humans. That's not collaborative. Children can sense this kind of power-hungry parenting and are likely to shut down out of fear or mirror that energy through power struggles. In both cases, you as the parent will be more likely to flex your power even harder. And that's just going to move you both further and further from the teaching moment. This is when we often wind up modeling behaviors that are not consistent with the family's values. We can't empower changes in our homes through hypocrisy. We have to embody the core family values even when our children are struggling with them. We have to use challenging moments to have tough, collaborative conversations.

That's why *communication* is one of my core values. It's the principle that I stand on and I think it's where I shine most in my parenting. That being said, this certainly was not always the case. And even after years of learning, using effective communication can sometimes still feel like a foreign language.

Still, I have come a long way since I started this journey toward better communication almost five years ago. At the end of my oldest daughter's kindergarten year, she and I decided to pull her out of public school and start homeschooling. I had no idea how much this decision would change my communication style for the better. She had spent the greater half of the year away from me for about six hours out of each day, so that meant we were going to be spending much more time together. Because of this, I chose to go through a process with her called *de-schooling*. It's a pretty loaded topic, but basically de-schooling is just taking some time away from any formal or structured learning to transition between traditional schooling and homeschooling. De-schooling creates an opportunity to reconnect with your child, build a foundation, help them acclimate to being out of school, and create a healthy environment for learning at home. During this time, we basically just focused on reinforcing our bond, establishing our values, and understanding our rhythms and routines.

And it's in this time that we had a lot of opportunities for communication. All day long we would just play and talk. (Ironically, at this same time I was learning the importance of effective communication in therapy, so I began applying this skill in our day-to-day interactions.) This was an incredible time in our lives. But it was also a bit shocking because the more we talked, the more I realized that there was a lot about her that I didn't know. It became very clear to me that I was living with a tiny stranger! I mean, I thought I knew her, but the more we communicated, the more I realized that, *damn*, I had been missing out on genuinely getting to know this awesome little creature! And I also noticed something that I now teach in my community: when we communicate with intention, it creates a much safer space to build connection, intimacy, and trust. So if you have a desire to strengthen your communication just like I did five years ago, I'd like to invite you to practice the following skills.

Using Silence

There's only one gift left to open! You see the excitement on your child's face and then it suddenly hits you that you totally forgot

10 Communication

to get the one gift he asked for. And in ten seconds the party goes from great vibes to a complete nightmare. Your son didn't get the one birthday gift he coveted and it may be the biggest tantrum you've seen since the huge fidget spinner catastrophe back in 2016. You didn't know he had more "flail on the ground" in him, but there he is, flopping around like a fish out of water on the kitchen floor. He's had it up to here with you! He says you don't listen to him and that you care more about his little brother than you care about him. You're just the meanest parent in the entire world! At least that's what he's spewing from his mouth at the highest volume you've ever heard him speak at. With a gentle tone, you start offering possible solutions, but it only seems to heighten the tantrum. Now you're starting to lose your cool. You just want it to stop, and despite knowing the moment will pass, you just want to fix it right this second.

So what do you do? *Nothing.* You do absolutely nothing. Don't talk. Don't teach. Don't try to discipline. Just close your mouth and get present with the moment. Resist the urge to fly in and defend your parental awesomeness with a list of ways you are, in fact, not the meanest parent on the planet. Don't take this as an opportunity to remind him that you love him as much as his brother. Unnecessary words are just not going to be received in the heat of the tantrum. Fight the desire to fix this moment. This moment is here to teach you both. Instead, ask yourself if you can sit with his discomfort. Can you remind yourself that teaching and discipline is more effective when both you and your child are calm? Can you model the calm that you want to see in your child so that he can learn to regulate himself? And can you take a moment to see the world through his eyes before you make a decision on how to respond? This is a great exercise to practice refraining from acting impulsively and powering over your child. It allows you to put some space between the action and your response. It gives you time to reflect, think more critically, and most importantly, communicate with empathy and compassion. Sometimes, our silence communicates more than our words ever could.

Using Active Listening

When our kids are talking to us, it's their turn to have the microphone, not ours. It's no small thing for your child to feel safe enough to come to you with their thoughts, ideas, and opinions. This is sacred! (It still blows my mind that my oldest actually still wants to talk to me about her day.) We can honor and cherish that level of trust and strive to keep it intact by consistently holding space for our children to express themselves. We can give them our attuned presence by practicing *active listening*. Active listening is about focusing your attention on your child's thoughts and words. The more you actively listen, the more you get to know your child and the closer you become. And the bonus is that as your child begins to feel securely attached, they'll get to know themselves better, as well. They'll feel more confident in their thoughts and beliefs. They'll be empowered to make decisions that are beneficial to your home dynamic.

Now I know this is easier said than done! Sometimes it's hard to just sit and listen to things that we don't agree with or to things that we have a desire to fix. You care about your children, so of course you want to help them! But our kids don't always need us to rush in with teaching and fixing. We model great behaviors all day. We model how to respond to frustrations and disappointments. And we model our beliefs and values to them as well. They get to witness our problem solving, our manners, and our patience throughout the day, so don't panic and assume you have to take every small opportunity to lecture them about those things.

Reflecting

The tool I use most to show my daughter that I am actively listening is *reflecting*. I go to this tool first because it requires very little input from me. (Remember: when you're actively listening, the less you contribute, the better.) So I try really hard and bite my tongue until my daughter is done sharing. At that point, I like to verbally reflect back what I heard to show her that I was listening. This exercise gives her an opportunity to "see" her thoughts. This is actually really powerful. Similar to writing or journaling, when we "see" our thoughts reflected back to us, it's an opportunity to effectively process them. Now, this is not intended to mean that you should repeat what they said word for word. Of course, if your child responds well to that kind of long-winded monologue, go for it, but if your child is anything like mine this will seem forced, contrived, and disingenuous. Instead, try just repeating a few things that they said back to them.

Let's say your son went on a ten-minute rant about how his best friend stole his toy at daycare, and the last thing he said was, "… and I don't want to be friends with him anymore." Instead of jumping in and saying, "Oh, but he's your best friend. You'll get over it," or "But he gave the toy back. Can't you forgive him?" You could just say, "Okay, you don't want to be friends with Johnny anymore. Thank you for sharing." This is how reflecting, rather than responding, lets them know that you are there to hold space for their thoughts. This will keep you from crossing any mental boundaries and powering over them. Remember: our children's thoughts are not dangerous. They only become dangerous over time when your children don't have a safe space to express and process them.

Asking Empowering Questions

You can also ask questions to go deeper. When done in an organic way, asking empowering questions can make space for more insightful and thought-provoking conversations. In these moments, we can go beyond just witnessing our children's thoughts— we can then give them an opportunity to explore their thoughts even further. This type of exploration is what helps them develop their own inner voices.

I typically like to ask three kinds of questions:

1. **Questions about their feelings.** Examples: *"How did you feel when Johnny took your toy?"; "What do you do when you feel sad?"*

2. **Questions that continue a story.** Examples: *"What happened after Johnny took your toy?"; "How did you respond to that?"; "What did your teacher say?"*

3. **Questions about their thoughts.** Example: *"What do you think would have happened if Johnny had asked for your toy?"*

The goal is to ask questions that allow them to think a bit more critically and to give them a chance to develop their own mindsets. It may be a scary thought for some, but our children are their own people with their own journeys. It is easy to forget this when we are so very responsible for them. It's a weird dynamic. But if we want our kids to grow up trusting themselves, we have to be willing to watch them write their own stories. We have to resist the urge to power over them with our own thoughts and opinions. Of course, we can model behaviors and share our opinions with them but ultimately they will decide who they are. If we want them to have positive self-images, we have to show them that we are comfortable with who they are, and we can do that by giving them a chance to share and process their own thoughts.

So even in our questioning, we can make sure we are not sneakily imposing our opinions on them. I'm guilty of asking questions with the goal of swaying my child's opinion. But this is just a passive-aggressive way of discrediting her voice. Here's an example of what I'm saying: "How do you think he felt?" empowers your child to think about the other person. On the other hand, "Don't you think that made him sad?" manipulates your child to agree with your thoughts and assumptions. Those thoughts and assumptions could be completely appropriate and you could be spot-on with your opinion, but when you ask questions with the primary goal of changing their mind rather than to understand, the child is robbed of the opportunity to develop those thoughts organically. Remember: when you ask questions, focus on empowering, not manipulating.

Making Recommendations

Once you've listened actively, asked deeper questions, and reflected what you've heard, you may be inclined to share your thoughts, opinions, or advice. This won't be everyone's preference and we don't necessarily have to use these moments as teaching moments. But if you do decide to give advice, there is an intentional way to do it.

Like with everything else, I don't leave giving advice up to chance. I have some scripts for empowering conversations. Why? Because it's not second nature for me. It isn't for a lot of us. If you have a brain full of ways to bark orders and absolutely no language for making recommendations, which do you think you'll be most likely to choose? It's a no-brainer. Having scripts that you can lean on will give you a fighting chance at speaking to your child with respect and humility. So let's make some scripts! Of course, I'll share some of my own, but making your own is super powerful. Here's the formula.

Step 1: Lead with Compassion

If you want to make sure your child still feels safe enough to really hear your constructive advice or teaching, you absolutely have to lead with compassion. Before you address anything, address your own energy. If you are irritated, bothered, or angry and you try to make recommendations from that space, your child will feel that. Instead, take a deep breath and open the conversation with compassion. It will soften you both.

Step 2: Get Consent

In order for our children to own and embody our core family values well into their adult lives, they need to have a certain willingness to do so. They have to choose those values. Values cannot be forced on our children without an increased risk of adverse effects in adulthood. If we want our children to *own* the family values, as parents we need to ease them onto our children in moments when they are receptive to receiving them. And the easiest way to figure out their receptivity level is to simply ask them about it.

Phrases for getting consent:

"Are you open?"

"Can we talk?"

"Can I share something with you?"

"Would you like to hear my point of view on this topic?"

"I have something to say. Is that cool with you?"

"May I borrow your ears for a second?"

How can you open a conversation with consent? What is a script that your child may respond well to? Make it as personal to your family as possible.

Step 3: Take a Step Back When Necessary

If your children do not give consent, consider what pressing on with the conversation will communicate to them. It will probably show them you don't respect their voice. What would happen if, instead, you thanked them for honoring their truth in the moment and simply asked them when a better time to talk would be? If they are resisting, whatever you're trying to teach probably won't be received anyway. Take their resistance as an opportunity to connect with them first, and then return to this process when you are both open.

Step 4: Offer Gentle Advice

I think it's important for our children to hear values mentioned as often as possible, even if they are written somewhere for everyone to see. The more conversations you have about values, the more ingrained those values will become in the family's culture. So before making a recommendation, I suggest reiterating the value to preface where the recommendation is coming from. This is how you shift the energy from your child working against you to your child working with you. When you remind your child of the value, you soften their receptivity. You're not trying to be the big mean parent. On the contrary, you're there to help them remember the values you all came up with when you created your family's mission statement.

Phrases for Mentioning the Value

"We value _____."

"Remember, _____ is important to us."

"_____ makes us all feel safe."

Think of ways that you can gently revisit your family's core values. What is a script that your child may respond well to? Make it as personal to your family as possible.

Step 5: Make the Recommendation

Once you've gotten consent and revisited the value, it's time to share your recommendation with your child. Remember, this is an empowering statement. You are not the all-knowing Wizard of Oz! The more humbly you approach your recommendation, the more compassionate it will sound to your child. Remember: parenting is leadership and it starts with you. So try to use communication that is less definitive and more connected, curious, and collaborative.

Phrases for Making Recommendations

"I wonder if _____."

"I think/believe _____."

"What if _____."

"Could _____ be true too?"

"What do you think about _____?"

Think of ways that you can make recommendations when your child is having a difficult time upholding family values. What is a script that your child may respond well to? Make it as personal to your family as possible.

Step 6: Encourage Critical Thinking

If your child is receptive to your feedback, give them the opportunity to work with you to strategize better behaviors for the future. You can tell them what to do or, instead, you can give them an opportunity to think of their own solutions first.

Step 7: Trust the Process

If you are living your family values, using positive discipline, and setting clear boundaries, you are doing your job. In fact, that's the only way making recommendations to your child will work. Of course, your child won't take gentle nudging seriously if you're not modeling appropriate behavior and setting boundaries yourself. But if you are, don't panic when they resist. It's a part of the process!

They are learning the values alongside so many other things. This will take time. And while it can be tempting to jump down their throats when they use words you don't like, roll their eyes, or leave the milk out on the countertop, you are here to support them through this process. That's really hard to do if you are talking *at* them rather than *to* them.

Examples of Recommendation Scripts

Here some scripts for making recommendations to your child.

Scenario 1

While sharing the events of her school day, Susan's daughter, Layla, told her she called her friend "stupid." Susan asked her to find another word, but her child dug her heels in even harder and started to explain why she thought her friend was so stupid. Once Layla stopped talking, Susan proceeded with the following script:

> Susan: *"Thank you for sharing that! It sounds like she really hurt your feelings? I understand. I know hugs make you feel better. Would you like one?"* (Starting with compassion.)
>
> Layla: *Yes!*
>
> Susan: *"Do you just want me to listen right now or is it okay if I share my thoughts?"* (Getting consent.)
>
> Layla: *"Sure, go ahead!"*
>
> Susan: *"You know we really value freedom of expression and I love that you feel comfortable telling me about your day in your own words. And we also value kindness."* (Mentioning the value.)
>
> *"I think there was a way to really express your anger with some kinder words."* (Making the recommendation.)
>
> *"What could you have said that would have let your friend know what you were feeling?"* (Encouraging critical thinking.)

Layla: *"I could have told her that I was really mad at her for not picking me to be her partner."*

Susan: *"Do you think she would have understood your feelings a bit better with those words?"*

Layla: *"Probably!"*

Scenario 2

Damian's son, Jamison, kept forgetting to do his homework. On the way home from school, Damian decided to address it.

Damian: *"Jamison, I know that you have a lot on your plate right now. You have soccer and gymnastics, and you still have school work. I got an email from your teacher about your homework."* (Starting with compassion.)

"Would you like to talk about that right now?" (Getting consent.)

Jamison: *"No."*

Damian: *"I respect your decision. This is something I'd like to discuss eventually. I'd like you to tell me a time that works for you. I'm not willing to ignore this for too long."* (Taking a step back.)

When our kids make mistakes, especially those that don't involve safety, they still deserve our patience. Sometimes all they need is a calm, collaborative conversation with some empowering recommendations.

In those moments can you lean them back in the direction of your core values? Absolutely. *And* you can use empowering conversations to do it without compromising the relationship.

Communicating through Play

So where do you begin with this stuff? What if your child struggles with articulating themself? What if you don't have the best communication skills yourself? How do you grow this skill together? Well, one of the most effective strategies is to not wait until communication is necessary to practice it. That's why I recommend using games to get more comfortable communicating with your children. Games are a lighthearted way to build a really valuable skill. Consistently practicing your communication when you are both regulated and open will make communication in tougher moments much easier. Here is a list of games you can use to help you both practice communication:

- **21 Questions.** Alternate taking turns asking each other questions. It's such a simple game but it's a great way to get to know your child. Be sure to only ask questions that your child is comfortable answering. This isn't a time to be intrusive. I can ask my older daughter deeper questions, but my four-year-old just wants to talk about her favorite fruit. That's okay! That's still important information and she still gets a chance to feel empowered and heard!

- **Never Have I Ever.** This game is a really fun way to see what similarities and differences you have! You hold up five fingers and say something you've never done, using the sentence, "Never have I ever _____." You'll say something you've never done that you aren't sure if the other person hasn't done. For instance, you wouldn't say, "Never have I ever done gymnastics" if your daughter is already in gymnastics. But something like, "Never have I ever dreamed in black and white" would be something you may not actually know! If the other person has done it, they'll put a finger down.

- **Would You Rather?** This either-or game helps you learn your child's preferences. You just take turns asking each other to choose between two options. Sometimes we'll keep it simple in my house, like choosing between eating two different meals. Other times our questions can get really complex. "Would you rather live in the Caribbean all by yourself or live in the Arctic with your friends and family?"

- **Nopes and Dopes.** We typically do this at the end of the day as a recap! This is our family's opportunity to share the highs and lows of the day. We take turns sharing a "nope" (something you didn't like) and then sharing a "dope" (something you thought was awesome).

- **Conversation Starters or Table Talks.** You can use conversation starters to go deeper with your kids. You can start a conversation jar with deeper questions that you and your kids can pull from or you can purchase conversation starter packs online. If you choose to buy them, they typically offer a range of topics. However, coming up with your own questions and creating your own cards is a great way to get your children more interested in participating!

Here are some journal prompts for improving communication:

- What is your level of competency with the five communication skills mentioned in this chapter (using silence, using active listening, reflecting, asking empowering questions, and making recommendations)? Which of these do you feel confident with and which are challenging?

- How can you practice those challenging skills? What communication game might work for your child? What other communication ideas do you have?

Part 3

The Intentional Parenting Toolkit

Alright, now let's talk about my intentional parenting tools. Having some quick positive discipline strategies can make it a lot easier to avoid passive and punitive parenting approaches, so in this part of the book I've compiled a list of the top six intentional parenting tools that I like to use. Interestingly, it always feels like I use a million different tools all day long, but really they're all just creative versions of these same six tools. If you watch my positive discipline videos on my social media channels, you'll notice that I pretty much just say the same six things a million different ways! Pretty cool, right? Gosh, I wish someone would outline those six strategies into an intentional parenting toolkit. Oh wait, I did! Read on!

As you read through this part of the book, I don't want you to think these are the only tools available to be an intentional parent—they definitely are not! You are the true expert on what your family needs and you're going to know what works for your family way better than me, so these tools are just a starting point. This book is about you. It's not about forcing, coercing, or manipulating your children into "doing" things. The goal with intentional parenting is to create a mutually respectful relationship between you and your child, and my hope is that that's exactly what these tools will help you do. Think of what you'll find in this section not as tools to "fix" bad behaviors, but as techniques you can use to model compassionate, fair, and appropriate behaviors. If you do that, your kids will come along for the ride in their own authentic ways.

11

You Can't Do a Don't
(Redirection)

As you move through your intentional parenting journey, there are an almost infinite number of scenarios you might encounter, and you may not feel prepared to deal with them all, but there is a tool that can be highly impactful: *redirection*.

What Is Redirection?

Redirection is the process of simply directing your child from one behavior to another, more appropriate behavior. It's the antithesis to just yelling "Stop!" Rather than focusing on what your child *can't* do, you focus on what they *can* do, instead. In a nutshell, redirection simply says this: "I'm not willing to let you do this, but you can do that." It allows for flexibility. It allows both you and your child to get your needs met. It honors the decision your child is trying to make while honoring the limits you're trying to set. That's why I like to call this tool the *power struggle diffuser*. It softens your *and* your child's defenses and puts you both in a more collaborative state.

"I won't let you do this" on its own leaves very little room for critical thinking or creativity. It's just like saying "No." If it's not a genuine nonnegotiable, it's extremely punitive and can breed very polar, all-or-nothing thinking. However, when you add "But you can do that," or even better, "What can we do instead?" you leave room for so many possibilities. You give yourself and your child an opportunity to work together to find creative solutions. Just saying "No" isn't all that realistic if you really think about it. It grinds my gears when people say, "I get it, but your kids are going to have to hear 'no' sometimes in the 'real world'." It's true, every situation and relationship has boundaries and levels of rigidity. As I mentioned in the previous chapter, I don't stray away from boundaries. But it's also true that most healthy relationships and situations have flexibility. Even as adults, "No" is often not the only option. With some critical thinking, there's usually a way to get your needs met while respecting the needs of others. The same can be true for your children. Let's use spitting bubbles as an example. If this doesn't go against your values and isn't nonnegotiable then there's room for flexibility. (Even if it is gross as hell!) "No, you can't blow spit bubbles at the dinner table. It's not really the appropriate place because we're trying to eat. After dinner you can blow them to your heart's content in the sink." They get to blow their bubbles and the rest of the family gets to eat without their stomachs turning.

Now you may think letting them do the action will increase the likelihood that they'll do it again and at inappropriate times. I'm not saying that's not possible, but remember that when we collaborate with our children and show them that their desires are also important, they will be much more willing to cooperate with us. And let's be honest, most circumstances aren't really black and white. There's often nuance and flexibility in regard to what is and isn't considered appropriate. This is called *situational appropriateness* and it's a learnable skill, even for kids. For example, do you hug your best friend? Probably! Would you hug a stranger without consent? I hope not! Do I drop F-bombs? Sometimes, but I probably wouldn't do so during a parent-teacher conference.

(Then again, knowing myself, maybe I would!). The point is that whether something is appropriate or not often can be situational. And you can teach your children this through redirection. Hitting a friend with a shovel? Inappropriate. Patting the sand with the shovel instead? Appropriate. Saying "shit" in church? Maybe that goes against the family's values. Saying "shit" at home? Maybe you're cool with that. Watching funny videos with your girlfriend in the bedroom? Maybe a no-go. But doing the same thing out in the living room? No problem!

Here are three strategies I like to use to implement redirection:

1. **Set limits compassionately.** Are you going to set limits? Absolutely. You will still say things like, "I'm not willing to let you ____" or "You can't ____." But *how* you set those limits can make all the difference. That may mean offering a warm voice. It could also mean relating to their situation by using phrases like, "I understand," "I hear you," "That makes sense," "I love that," or "I totally get it."

2. **Redirect them to another behavior.** Sure, you need to set limits, but it can be helpful to give your child other options. Just as important as teaching your child what *not* to do is guiding them toward what *to do*. Rather than just focusing on what they can't do, give them something that they *can* do that's still respectful of your values. It's also important that you understand what your child actually wanted to do in the first place in order for the redirection to be effective. If your child desires play, telling them to sit down is not an intentional redirection. If your child desires noise, asking them to quiet down is not an intentional redirection. It doesn't mean that you won't ever ask your kids to sit down or lower their voices, but that just wouldn't be considered redirection. In instances where there's a bit less flexibility, you might need to use a different approach, but when we redirect, it's important to still *collaborate* to get their needs met.

3. **Whenever possible, allow space for their feedback and influence.** "You can do this instead" is great, but asking them "What else can we do?" encourages your child to think critically and problem solve. Asking for feedback is a great strategy because it gets their brains off thinking about the limit and onto making a decision.

Here's an example of how I've put these strategies into action. Recently, my four-year-old was making a lot of noise while I was on an important call. I told her "I love how freely you express yourself. Can you cluck like a chicken in your room until I finish this call?" When I tried to redirect my daughter to another room, she resisted. I thought she just needed to make noise. But then I used curiosity and asked, "Why do you want to stay in my room?" to which she replied, "Because I'm a chicken! Look at me!" She was dancing in the mirror, shaking her arms, and clucking. Then it hit me: she wasn't just having fun being a chicken, she was having fun *watching herself* be a chicken. So I said to her, "Don't be stingy! The mirror in the hallway has to see your chicken dance, too. Go, go, go!" I could have also given her options like "Which mirror do you think needs to see your chicken dance next? The hall or the bathroom?"

Redirection Scenarios

One of my favorite gentle parenting adages is "You can't do a don't!" If you only say, "Don't jump on the couch," you're not actually guiding your children toward more appropriate behaviors. Instead, you might say, "I'm not willing to let you jump on the couch. But let's see how high you can jump on the floor, instead." Let's illustrate this with a few scenarios:

- **Scenario 1:** Your toddler is playing nicely in the sandbox with a new playmate they just met at the park. They are working diligently on a sandcastle when all of a sudden you notice your child becoming frustrated. You see the anger boiling up and you suspect that things may escalate. Armed with a shovel, they raise the shovel to hit the other child. You try to stop them, but the shovel makes contact with the other child before you can intercede.

- **Scenario 2:** Your six-year-old becomes fixated on a new word they learned at school. It's one of *those* words. Though they haven't said it to you yet, they can't get enough of it when they're with their friends. Finally, after weeks of embedding the word into their vocabulary, you hear it for the first time. When? Last Sunday... at church... during prayer. (Talk about perfect timing!)

- **Scenario 3:** You come home from work, and as you're sitting down to rest your feet you hear someone laughing hysterically. Your teenager does not laugh hysterically. But you know who does? Their girlfriend! You open the bedroom door to find them sitting on the bed, scrolling through social media.

In each of these situations, there are several possible disciplinary routes to take, but they're not all effective. A passive parent wouldn't do much to address the behavior at all, while an authoritarian parent would address the behavior with force but miss out on the opportunity to use connection, communication, curiosity, and collaboration. An intentional parent, however, would use redirection to encourage their child to move away from the inappropriate behavior and steer them toward something more appropriate.

Let's take a closer look at the examples again, but this time with some redirections:

Scenario 1: Rather than storming over to the toddler and saying, "Hey, don't hit!"

You may say, "Hitting hurts your new friend. How about we use the shovel to make a big sand pile, instead?"

Now, if you're thinking, "Wait, so we're going to let them keep the shovel even though they were trying to hit?" My answer is "yes"! When a child breaks a rule, it doesn't always mean they're not ready for the situation. Oftentimes it just means they may need a stronger boundary. You may need to sit a bit closer so they can't hurt the other child if they get frustrated again, but the first option doesn't have to be taking the shovel. There are just so many more intentional choices. Remember, you are trying to use intentional parenting to *teach* your child, not punish them. And how can you teach your child the situationally appropriate way to use a shovel if they don't get to use the shovel? So the solution in this scenario is to stay close to ensure that target practice doesn't resume and then offer a fun alternative!

Scenario 2: As you're sitting in church and you hear your child say something you wouldn't have expected to hear from them in a million years, reflect on what's happening for you internally. Are you confused? Are you angry? Are you humored and embarrassed at the same time? Is this word genuinely an issue for you or is it simply the place that made the word inappropriate? If you find that the word doesn't go against your values but was just a matter of "wrong place, wrong time," you could use this opportunity to really empower your child. You might say the following:

"I see you really like that word…" (connection and communication)

"… I wonder if we can find a more appropriate time to use it." (curiosity and collaboration)

Scenario 3: It may be infuriating to find your teenager and their girlfriend snuggled up on the bed. Instead of overreacting, you might come up with a fair alternative. In this instance, and especially if it's the first time it's

11 You Can't Do a Don't

happened, you may pull your child to the side and redirect in the following way:

"Hey kiddo! You two sound like you're having a great time..." (connection);

"... I get that you're probably at a stage where you want more independence..." (curiosity)

"... but I'm not okay with you having her coming over when I'm not home..." (communication)

"... I'm also not okay with you two being in the bedroom. Let's talk about some more appropriate ways for her to visit. I'm certainly open to your suggestions and think we can find something that works for everyone." (collaboration)

In all three examples, limits are set, but the main difference between redirection and punishment is the heavy emphasis on collaboration. Punishment is entirely about inflating the parent and making the child "small." In contrast, redirection empowers your child and shows them that they deserve your trust. And children often rise or shrink to our beliefs about them. So by working with your child, you empower them. You are able to find solutions that don't require either of you to power over the other. This is why redirection is hands down one of my favorite intentional discipline tools. It's just so fair. And I like fair!

12

Safe and Sound
(Self-Regulation and Co-Regulation)

Have you ever heard the phrase "swimming against the current"? Well, I don't know much about the ocean, but it's my limited understanding that a rip current can pull you away from shore and so it's best not to try to swim against it. There's a swimming technique you can use to escape, but if you're a novice swimmer, your best bet is to just stay afloat until help comes.

I'm a visual person, so I can vividly imagine what I might look like if I ever faced a rip current. I can picture myself (a pretty terrible swimmer) fighting aggressively against waves that are stronger than me. I can see myself flailing around, trying to make my way back to shore… trying my hardest, but failing miserably. At that point, I might drift farther and farther away from the shore and lose hope. I think this is an effective metaphor for what happens in moments where our children are throwing tantrums and we attempt to fix their feelings ("It's okay!"), shut them down ("Stop crying!"), or correct the way they're expressing their emotions ("Use your words!"). Like the person fighting tirelessly against the current, we can move farther and farther from the shore. The shore represents safety, and that's where intentional discipline happens. The shore is the place where our children learn effective tools for managing their own anger, sadness, or distress. But with many children, the more you fight against their tantrums, the further you get from being able to give them that useful guidance. One of the most intentional ways to move through a tantrum is to offer your child's emotions safety by simply "staying afloat." Rather than trying to urgently rush through the moment, you get present, return yourself to a calm state, and ride it out until the waves subside.

What Are Self-Regulation and Co-Regulation?

This brings me to the most effective tools for managing tantrums in my tool belt: *self-regulation* and *co-regulation*. *Self-regulation* is the process of managing our own emotional states as we respond to experiences. Co-regulation prioritizes the in-the-moment need to return your child to a place of safety by first finding a place of physical safety for both of you, regulating yourself, and then inviting your child into your safe space and your own place of regulation. Co-regulation is the tool that will get you through those difficult moments without compromising connection, curiosity, collaboration, and communication. When our children are throwing tantrums, they need our support (acceptance and confidence) to help them manage their own emotional responses. But it's not a means to an end. The goal isn't just to help our children calm down or just to get them focused enough to make the bed or get out of the house on time. Co-regulation in and of itself *is* the goal. When your child is ranting and raving, sobbing uncontrollably, or covering their ears, they are likely in a *fight, flight, or freeze* mode. They do not learn emotional intelligence on their own, so it's important in these moments to try to stop everything else to the best of your ability and help them regulate themselves. Practically speaking, in order to co-regulate you need to first find a physical place where you will both feel safe, and then you become a "safe place" for them by regulating yourself, and then you invite them into this safe space so they can then learn to regulate themselves. The following sections explore these three steps a bit further.

Step 1: Creating Physical Safety

The first step in regulating emotions is creating safety by finding a physical space where you and your child can move through the emotions safely. This may mean you both have to leave the grocery store and go sit in your car until you've both found a peaceful place. Or you may need to remove your child from the birthday party and go to a quiet room where you can talk things over. If the four-year-old is running through the house and throwing things, you may need to take them to a more confined area where they can't throw things. Think of this safe place as a "container" where you can both move through the big feelings while doing minimal harm to things, others, or each other. When seeking a place of safety, consider what the safest nearby place may be where your child can do the least amount of harm. Also ask yourself what the safest space may be where *you* can do the least amount of harm. If you are around other people and feeling embarrassed by your child's behavior, *you* are more likely to do harm. If your child is physically raging in the living room where there are breakable items, *they're* more likely to do harm to themselves, to things, or even to other children. In order to start the process of co-regulation, everyone first needs to be in a safe place.

Step 2: Becoming the Safe Space (Self-Regulation)

If we are not embodying safety ourselves, our children will stay dysregulated for much longer than necessary. When they are panicking and freaking out, their brains, at a very primal level, are responding to perceived threats. It's our job to remind their nervous systems that they are safe. And we can't make them feel safe when we ourselves are dysregulated—they won't be receptive to their own co-regulation if we don't regulate ourselves first. Though we outlined how to move through your triggers in an earlier chapter, I want to outline what this might look like in the process of co-regulation. I use the acronym **S.A.F.E.** to explain this process. The following steps for regulating yourself require no words at all. Remember, your children are not using rational functioning, so little to no verbal communication will likely work best. Here is what the **S.A.F.E.** acronym means.

"**S**" (*See* what is happening.) You have to be a witness to the moment and detach yourself from immediate reactivity by simply noticing what is happening first. First, take note of what is going on in the moment and what is your child doing. Next, take note of how you are being triggered and how that feels in your body. If your child is not yet receptive to your words, you might say to yourself, "My child is screaming right now. I feel overwhelmed. My heart is starting to race."

"**A**" (*Accept* what is.) Resist the urge to make judgments. Let your observations be just that. There is no need to apply labels or stories to the moment. You might affirm to yourself, "This is okay," or "This moment will pass," or "I accept what 'is' in this moment."

"**F**" (*Find* your calming tool.) It's important to have strategies that calm your nervous system. Often, when we're triggered, we can feel disconnected from our physical bodies. Reconnecting to our bodies with a calming tool allows us to slowly transition from reactivity to responsiveness. I list some helpful calming tools at the end of this chapter; however, my number one go-to calming tool is deep breathing. It's the most accessible tool to use, regardless of where I am. Deep breathing gives me something to focus on while I'm slowing down my mental and physical processes.

"**E**" (Gently move into *empathy*.) This is how you begin to transition into co-regulation. Rather than forcing your child to calm down, simply show them that you are ready to support them. Let your openness be evident in your body language as you invite, rather than force, a shift in their energetic state. We open the door by opening our arms for them (both figuratively and literally), inviting them to be received. By doing this, we don't just calm our children's storms, we calm ourselves and invite them to experience that calm with us. We manage our emotional states and express an openness and willingness to support them as they try to manage their own emotions. The best way to show your children you are open is through empathy.

When your child is throwing a tantrum, they are experiencing feelings that need to be felt, not fixed. (I mean, they're called feelings, not fixings, right?) When you resist the urge to fight against the current, you give yourself and your child a fighting chance. So staying afloat during a tantrum just means opening yourself up and allowing their emotions to be seen and experienced. It's about *observing* rather than *judging* what you see and hear. It's about understanding their emotions. And that's exactly what they need when they are untethered and dysregulated—an opportunity to experience the full expression of their emotions with an understanding caretaker. Sometimes it requires acknowledging their emotions out loud. Sometimes it requires saying nothing at all. But they need to experience the emotions so that they can slowly learn to better regulate them. This is how they learn emotional intelligence. Think back to the redirection example of teaching a toddler how to use a shovel. Similar to that example, we cannot teach our children how to appropriately experience emotions if they're never allowed to express them in the first place.

When my daughter is throwing a tantrum or expressing big feelings, I find that the closer I lean toward empathy, the more aware of her own emotional state she becomes. However, the more I lean into trying to fix or correct her behavior, the further into the tantrum she goes. Sometimes I'll just sit, be quiet, and breathe. If empathetic language isn't being received, I resist the urge to do something and instead I just sit there silently and empathize with her in my head. That's it. And, ironically, this kind of inaction winds up being an extremely active and intentional practice. Do you know how much effort it can take to be able to notice their big feelings and still sit quietly in discomfort? It can be brutal. It takes courage, patience, and incredible strength. But it is through modeling the observation of their emotions that our children learn to observe their own emotions themselves. Plus, when I go inward and find empathy for the moment, I soften. And they recognize this softening and are more likely to slowly begin to mirror it.

I desire to teach my children emotional intelligence. And believe it or not, tantrums are like gold when it comes to building this skill! Emotional intelligence can be cultivated in these moments by allowing them to get comfortable experiencing their emotions and understanding them. In order to do that, I have to be their example. I have to take a deep breath, get present with my discomfort in the moment, allow myself to experience the fullness of their emotions, and seek to understand them. And that is why understanding their emotions is a practice that I'm committed to. It's something I've struggled with in the past and so I find it helpful to have some go-to phrases that are not rooted in sympathy, advice, consoling, or any of the other above-mentioned strategies. The following are purely observational, empathetic statements that serve as a way to prioritize holding space for their feelings. I'd like to share a few with you.

Empathetic phrases I say to my children if they are receptive to communication:

- I understand.
- I hear you.
- I see your big feelings.
- I imagine you are feeling _____ right now.

Empathetic phrases I say to myself if my children are not receptive to communication:

- This is big to her. (I got this from one of my amazing clients.)

- I can understand her feelings in this moment.
- Her feelings need space to be expressed.
- I can handle her big feelings.
- Her emotions are not bad, undesirable, or shameful.
- I have time for her big feelings.

Less Effective Strategies

When we don't lean into empathy, we miss the opportunity to hold space for our child's emotions. This can happen with even the gentlest of parents. We are all guilty of using well-meaning strategies that are simply not empathetic and do not hold space for our children's emotions. Here are some common strategies that, while seemingly effective in principle, can actually be more counterproductive than helpful if we don't lean into empathy first.

Sympathizing

When our children are crying or yelling, it can be tempting to move into sympathy. Sympathy is a form of compassion. It's the ability to feel what someone else is feeling. Sympathy can be really powerful in helping our children feel like they are not alone with their emotions. It shows them that emotions are universal. For that reason, it is important for our children to hear us say things like "I'm so sorry this happened to you" or "I'm really upset about that, too." It's comforting and increases connection. However, it does not teach a child the practice of witnessing their own emotions. If we don't first empathize, we run the risk of taking away their ability to sit with discomfort and work through it. There won't always be someone to sympathize with them. So we start with holding space for their emotions so they can thrive with or without sympathy. While it may be tempting to show your children that you feel what they're feeling, an emotional intelligence–based option may be to start with simply showing your child that you *understand* what they're feeling.

Advising

Maybe you're the advice parent. Maybe instead of sympathizing, your first instinct is often to coach them through their feelings.

"You can just get another toy."

"Let's try to take some deep breaths."

"If you just ask, she might share the doll."

These kinds of statements are great for helping your child find solutions, but your child's feelings are not problems and they don't need solutions. So when your child is overtaken by their big feelings, you do their emotions a disservice by skipping over the emotional roots and dealing only with the external symptoms.

Consoling

Maybe you tend to jump into comforting your child.

"It's okay. It's going to be alright."

Of course, you want to ensure that your child knows that their big feelings won't last forever. But again, use empathy first! Imagine losing your job or a loved one. I think back to when I lost my mom. Several people walked up to me and told me "it's going to be alright." And while I knew that rationally to be true, emotionally I just needed someone's presence. I needed safe spaces to feel my feelings. The rational, comforting conversations were much more palpable when they came from a place of empathy.

Let's not forget that our children's big feelings can feel just as overwhelming as those major losses might feel for us. They haven't had as many disappointments and letdowns in their lives.

And so they haven't had enough experiences to create a tolerance for different degrees of pain. So when their friend leaves the park, they can experience the full weight of grief (even though they just met them twenty minutes ago). When they expected to go to the beach for their birthday, but it rains, it can feel like the biggest letdown ever. And, quite frankly, it might literally be the biggest letdown up until that point in their life. Pain is relative to the person experiencing it. And just like our own grief, sadness, and sorrow all deserve time to be processed, so does theirs. Just like with sympathizing, comforting without first letting them have their feelings can rush the process.

Making Quick Judgments

Maybe you make quick judgments to try to resolve situations quickly.

"Somebody needs a nap!"

"Oh, she's just hungry."

Assumptions are the death of curiosity. And while there may be a genuine need that is commanding your attention, there's a superseding emotional need that needs to be addressed. Often in gentle parenting spaces I hear, "Meet the need and the tantrum will subside." Some people mistake this to mean that if you cater to the external need, the internal need will soften. And while laying down a dysregulated toddler for a nap might do just the trick, we aren't always in a position to meet external needs. There will be moments when they're not going to get what they want. Maybe you're thirty minutes from the restaurant and they can't eat right this second. Maybe they ripped their security blanket and you can't replace it at 9:00 at night. Maybe you have no control over their friend no longer talking to them. In these moments especially, your diagnoses of what's "wrong" won't matter more than being the strong tower there to support them as they experience their big feelings.

Using Positive Reinforcement

Maybe you interrupt tantrums with positive reinforcement or affirmations.

"I know you can do this."

"You can do hard things, I know you can try again."

This kind of positive coaching is great! Affirming our children is extremely powerful. However, it doesn't allow their feelings to be seen. When we try to force our children into a positive space, we reject what they are actually experiencing. A feeling that is not acknowledged only grows, festers, and eventually takes over. Feelings need empathy just as much as an empty stomach needs food. What would happen if you went too long without food? Eventually you would eat anything just to meet that need. The same is true of emotions. Eventually, children will do whatever needs to be done in order for their feelings to be seen and expressed.

Questioning

I'd like to share one more way parents swim against the current and struggle to express empathy and understanding, and it's actually *my* biggest struggle when my children are having big feelings—it's asking too many questions. It can be so difficult not to try to figure out what's wrong so you can remedy the situation. While curiosity is one of the most important elements of intentional parenting, we must seek to understand the feeling before trying to understand the circumstances. Sure, probing and questioning may be effective when your children are mildly upset. You may ask questions like "What are you feeling?" or "What happened?" but if the emotional waves are extremely tumultuous, this type of questioning can just put you further away from shore.

If my child is wailing on the floor, asking them "What's wrong?" doesn't matter in the moment. Whatever it is that they needed before the tantrum can wait because there is a superseding need: right now they need emotional support. We'll have time to figure out what's up once the waves of emotion have calmed a bit. But in the beginning, they just need my empathy.

Witnessing your child's emotions first will make those other tools, like sympathizing, consoling, advising, and asking questions, so much more effective in the long run. Not only do we want our children to know how to deal with tough situations, we also want them to know how to deal with the tough feelings that often come with them! And we can't do this until we move into an empathetic state.

Step 3: Co-Regulation (Inviting Them into Your Calm)

Once you've found a a safe physical space and are able to self-regulate from a place of empathy, your child will slowly start to mirror your energy. This is a great time to move into the co-regulation process and invite your child into the calm, empathetic state you have already brought yourself into. I use the acronym **S.O.U.N.D.** to explain this process.

"S" (*Slow* and gentle.) How can you show your child that their feelings aren't urgent or scary? Slow down! Show them there is no rush and no need to be afraid of the big feelings. Speak with a slow and gentle tone. Move your body more slowly. Model what it looks like to have a calm, regulated nervous system. If your child is scratching themself because they're having a hard time with their anxiety, gently hold their hands. If your child is screaming about how much they hate you, don't match their agitated tone. Instead, respond with a calm, reassuring presence.

Your child will slowly start to respond to your slow, gentle demeanor.

"O" (Use *one* or two phrases.) Keep your verbal communication to a minimum. As you both move through regulation, your child may slowly start to be open to words. But verbal communication can often do more harm than good when our children aren't in the ventral vagal state. So try to limit your verbal communication to just one or two reassuring phrases that can express safety to your child. Here are some of my favorites:

- You are safe.
- I'm right here.
- I won't leave you.
- You are not alone.
- I know.
- I've got you.

Ultimately, if they are not ready to hear your communication, try to trust that your silence and self-regulation can communicate safety on their own.

"U" (*Understand* their cues.) Pay close attention to your child's cues. As they learn to self-regulate, children may ride the emotional wave up and down a few times before finally calming themselves. Pay attention to the cues that come with this process and try to understand their responses to your presence in the situation.

"N" (*Nudge* them with a calming tool.) As you pay attention to their cues, you may want to consider using some calming tools. Sometimes your children may be super receptive to these tools and other times they may not. Children will access these tools when they are ready to do so. That's why I like to think of this as a "nudge," rather than a "push." If they're becoming more dysregulated when you tell them they are safe, back up and return to silence. If they are slow to respond to verbal communication, try nudging them with a calming tool. You might ask, "Hey, do you want to try taking some deep breaths?" and then see how they respond. You can only help them use their calming tools to whatever degree they'll allow. My oldest may not respond right away if I ask if she wants a hug; however, if I rub her back while she cries, she won't push away. For your child, maybe what works is turning off the lights or maybe you just model some deep breathing for them until they're ready to join in. Maybe you hum in their ear or turn on some gentle music. It's about meeting your child wherever they are, with whatever calming tool they are receptive to using.

"**D**" (*Do* it until they feel safe.) Self-regulating and co-regulating are not linear processes. You may need to move back and forth through these stages several times before the tantrum actually subsides. That's okay! Just commit to being patient and present. Be determined to stay with your child as long as possible, understanding that the more you both practice the easier it will get. Eventually they'll be able to do this on their own. (That's definitely the goal, right?!) But for now, we get to teach this process by becoming more aware and less reactive. It is in your stillness that you can offer safety to your children in moments of distress. This is how they will learn to regulate their own emotions—not through forced time-outs or taking their toys, and certainly not through punishment. Our children learn emotional intelligence through watching us regulate ourselves and consistently support them to do the same—that's it! This can take a lot of time, especially in the beginning, but with consistent practice both you and your children will grow and it will become easier for you both to guide yourselves back to shore, S.A.F.E and S.O.U.N.D.!

Helpful Calming Tools

As you consider what will be the most effective calming tools for you and your child, try to think about calming the senses: taste, smell, touch, sight, and sound. There are also physical tools and activities that help your child find a calmer state.

Taste: A cool glass of water or a nourishing snack can help calm the body and the mind.

Smell: Essential oils, scented candles, or scent diffusers can be helpful for creating a soothing environment.

Touch: A gentle massage or a back rub, hair brushing, scalp massage, gently squeezing and releasing hands, and hugs are all helpful tools you personally can use to help your child. If your child prefers to soothe themself through touch, physical tools like sensory swings, weighted blankets, sensory fidgets (pop-its, spinners, stress balls), soft objects (pillows, blankets, stuffed animals), fuzzy socks, sensory bins (rice, water, beads), bubble wrap, or play dough, slime, or Silly Putty can all be helpful.

Sight: Sunlight, calming lights, and even darkness can all help soothe frayed nerves.

Sound: Calming music, humming, singing, whispering, counting down aloud, and verbalized positive affirmations can all be helpful.

Physical: Activities like deep breathing, grounding (feet to the earth), lying on a cool surface (like a floor), pushing against a wall, hanging upside down, rocking back and forth, blowing bubbles, squeezing pillows, and self-massage can all be helpful. Sports-related activities like walking, jumping, or playing catch with a friend can also be effective.

13

"Let's Revisit This Later"
(Recaps and Storytelling)

As parents, we send small messages to our children about their behaviors all day long. We're like their coaches, and even the most lenient of us make requests or give some sort of guidance. And whether we are conscious of it or not, our children actually cooperate with us a significant amount throughout each day.

However, there are, of course, going to be "those moments" when your child is completely unreceptive to your teaching. (You know what moments I'm talking about.) It's usually when they are overstimulated or wrapped up in big emotions. It's those moments when you've struggled with bedtime for hours, going back and forth and having nighttime negotiations with a four-year-old. Or those moments when you spent a ton of money on birthday presents only for your child to lose their mind about the one gift they *didn't* get.

And in those moments it can be tempting for you to go full force with the discipline because these situations can be quite triggering. And because they are triggering, you probably won't be able to best articulate yourself to your children in an intentional way. Furthermore, they're probably a lot less likely to hear you in those moments. That's why it's important to resist the urge to discipline in those "triggered" moments because your child is more likely to turn their emotions outward and toward you or someone else, or inward toward themselves. In fact, when they are not receptive, the best thing you can teach them is patience and acceptance. Otherwise, you'll be wasting your time and more than likely feeding the situation in a negative way. No, thank you!

What Is Recapping and Storytelling?

So if you don't discipline in the heat of the moment, when *do* you discipline? You do it when both you and your child feel safe and sound. You do it once the waves of emotion have subsided. You do it during a recap! A recap is your opportunity to use storytelling to recall an earlier situation in hopes of teaching a specific lesson or encouraging a specific behavior. Most importantly, recaps are an opportunity for your child to tell you *their* interpretation of the situation so that *they* can teach you something as well.

When your child is dysregulated emotionally or energetically, it is extremely difficult for them to separate themselves from their behavior. This either puts them on the defense or induces shame. But when you come back to the situation after your child's emotions and energy are regulated, they're more detached from the behavior and can see their actions much more logically.

Think about when you're upset. It's a lot more difficult for you to think rationally. But once the moment has passed, you're able to review the situation with more logic. And even if you're still feeling defensive or shameful, it's probably much less so than it was in the heat of the moment. Once a situation has calmed down, it's much easier to see someone else's point of view, reflect on mistakes, and come up with better options for the future. The same is true for our children!

If your child is overstimulated and they won't go to bed, it's probably not the best time for a lecture on the importance of rest. Deal with the overstimulation first and then talk to them about rest the following day during a recap. If your child is sobbing because they didn't get something they really wanted, it's probably not the best time to teach them about gratitude. Deal with the emotions first and then teach them about gratitude during a recap. Does the lesson still get taught? Yes it does, but at a better time.

So in those moments when you have that strong desire to correct them, ask yourself: "Will I just be heard or will I actually be understood?" Can you communicate the lesson using connection, curiosity, and collaboration? If not, recap it later. Is your child even open to your communication, connection, curiosity, and collaboration? If not, recap it later. Wait until you are both regulated before disciplining. And bonus points if you can wait to discipline at a time when you're both feeling playful or joyful. It's often during play that our children learn the best.

How to Use Recaps

So how do you use recaps to revisit those more challenging experiences while also teaching a specific lesson? Well, there are four important criteria for an effective recap, and it should come as no surprise to find that those elements are *connection, curiosity,* and *collaboration,* and *communication,*!

Connection

Recaps happen best when you and your child feel connected to each other. Sometimes I'm able to connect with my child right after the moment has calmed down. Other times, I wait until later moments in our routine when we are typically connected. Think about the moment when you feel closest to your child—that may be during the bedtime routine, in the morning, during bath time, or even in the car. Whenever that moment is, I think of it as the "recap zone." This is a safe space. This is when you and your child feel most connected and your child will be more open to a recap. You'll also be more likely to discipline compassionately in the recap zone.

Communication

Make sure that your communication is full of kindness. Get consent when necessary; speak to your child in the way that they feel most safe and avoid blaming or shaming language. Though I can be very animated, I try to remain as neutral as possible in my recaps. I just stick to the facts and avoid emotionally charged language. The original situation is for the big emotions, but the recap is my opportunity to connect those feelings to logic, rationalization, and positive behavior.

Curiosity

As you begin to retell the story of what happened, make sure that your story is full of curiosity. Allow your child to fill in some of the blanks and share what happened in their own words. Ask questions like the following:

- Do you remember what happened after that?
- Do you recall what you said?
- What were you feeling when that happened?
- What were you needing?

Collaboration

Once you've retold the story of what happened, collaborate on future possibilities. It can be tempting to just tell your child what to do the next time. (If they're younger, you'll probably need to.) But remember that you want your child to own the behavior. So if they are developmentally able to collaborate on coming up with more appropriate behaviors, allow them to do that with you. Try these approaches:

- "Instead of doing that, next time would you like to try _____ or _____?"

- "What could you do instead next time?"
- "What can I do to support you next time?"
- "How can we work together to get both of our needs met in a realistic way?"

That last example is pretty important. Finding solutions for future challenges has to be mutually beneficial in order for you and your child to both feel empowered. Furthermore, it has to be realistic if you want it to stick. Your child may want you to sleep with them, but if you have to take care of your night routine when they go to bed, it's probably not going to work long term. But the great thing about collaborative recaps is that you can keep coming back to them. You don't have to get everything figured out in one sitting. There's no urgency to "fix" the behavior. Just show your child that you are confident that eventually you'll both find a solution that works for everyone. I also use storytelling every single day in my parenting. It's so ingrained in the culture of my home that my kids expect it. Sometimes, when we are having a tough time or not seeing eye to eye, I remind them that we can always figure it out later. "Later" is typically during our recap.

The Fitness Watch

Here's an example of a recent recap experience in our house. My older daughter is probably one of the most empathetic people I've ever met. She can really feel other people's emotions. Because of that, I have to be extremely careful about how and when I discipline her. We've both agreed that some conversations are better held when we're both calm. And she doesn't miss an opportunity to hold me to that. If there's even the slightest bit of irritation in my voice, she shuts down. She becomes far less receptive and sometimes even combative. That's exactly what happened today. She randomly saw a fitness tracker watch and wanted one. I told her I'd get her one and she was ecstatic. Unfortunately, that joy was short lived when she realized I didn't mean I'd get her one *today*. She was really only mildly disturbed and she probably would have responded well to a compassionate "I understand you're upset. Let's figure out when you can get the watch." I wish I could say I chose compassion, but I did not. I was so triggered. Why was she even mad at me? What the heck did I do? Who asks for something that expensive and expects it right that second? She's being such a little diva!

We all have moments when we can't stand our kids' behaviors. And that was one of those moments. I did not check in with my body. I did not use a quick calming tool. When those thoughts popped into my head, I tried to mask my frustration with a restrained "Sorry, kiddo." I might as well have rolled my eyes because she saw right through my act. And that is when the tantrum ensued. There were a few unkind words directed at her sister and me, a bit of car door slamming, and tears, of course. Now you know at this point I wanted to bring the thunder and release the kraken! But I resisted. I just drove home, took deep breaths, and offered compassionate responses when I could genuinely do so. And guess what? The storm didn't last forever. When we got inside, I offered to hold her hand (physical touch is a calming tool for her) and she relaxed a bit and then she was ready to talk... finally. Though she was still a bit teary-eyed, she was receptive to my compassion. And that is a perfect time to recap. As the tears dried, she climbed onto my lap. As we snuggled up on the floor, we began to recap. It went a bit like this:

> Me: "*Are you open?*
>
> Her: "*Yes.*"
>
> Me: "*Good. If at any point you start to feel like I'm talking at you and not to you, please let me know. Earlier, you didn't get the fitness watch. How'd you feel in that moment?*"
>
> Her: "*I don't know.*"
>
> Me: "*I wonder if you felt sad. Is that true?*"
>
> Her: "*No. I was really angry.*"

15 "Let's Revisit This Later"

Me: *"Thank you for sharing your feelings with me! I imagine that it was really hard not being able to get something you were so excited about. If I'm being honest, I recall brushing it off like it was no big deal. But I can see that it was a big deal and I'm so sorry I didn't honor your feelings. Do you remember what happened after that?"*

Her: *"I got really mad and said something mean."*

Me: *"Yup. And do you think that might have impacted your sister?"*

Her: *"Probably."*

Me: *"Sounds like you're paying attention to your sister's feelings. That's powerful. How do you think she felt?"*

Her: *"Sad?"*

Me: *"I think so. It didn't feel good to hear you say those unkind words to me, and I imagine she felt something similar. We'll ask her later. Either way, I love you so much. You are not a bad child and I think expressing yourself is really important. My concern is that we all have to feel safe around each other. What can we do next time so that you can express yourself and everyone can also feel safe?"*

Her: *"I don't know."*

Me: *"Well, I wish I knew how upset you were about the watch so we could just talk about it and figure it out. But you didn't tell me. What's something you could have said so that I could be aware of your feelings?"*

Her: *"I could have said, 'I'm angry' instead of doing the unkind stuff."*

Me: *"I think that's a great answer. When you share your feelings rather than showing your feelings, it's much easier to work together! Let's try that next time. If that doesn't work, I know we can figure something out that does."*

This is how our recaps always go. We connect when we both feel safe and regulated; I communicate without blame or shame; I ask questions and remain curious; and we work together to come up with more appropriate behaviors.

Now, if you're thinking, "Okay, that sounds great, but when do you make her say she's sorry?" And the honest answer is *never*. See, when you use force, your child's apology has very little to do with compassion and a lot more to do with blind compliance. But when you use recaps and storytelling, your child will be much more open to you encouraging accountability. With the recap you help process the event, model accountability by taking ownership of any of your ineffective behaviors, and most importantly, you help them calm their nervous systems. At that point, the triggering event is no longer threatening, and your child can better understand the need for an apology because their brain has quite literally returned to a more rational state.

Here's some language I use to encourage accountability:

Open-ended questions:

- How can we repair what happened?
- How can we fix this?
- What can you say to show your sister you still care?
- When would you like to apologize?
- I know that saying you're sorry is hard sometimes. How can I support you?

Yes-or-no questions:

- Do you think saying you're sorry could help?
- Are you ready to apologize?
- Do you think you can apologize to your sister?
- Would you like to apologize now?

15 "Let's Revisit This Later"

Recapping and storytelling are the tools that support the co-regulation process. It's the answer for skeptics who say, "You helped them with their feelings, but what about the behavior?" Yes, we are to guide and support our children toward value-based behaviors, but we do it in a way that is beneficial to their brain development and well-being. We don't compromise emotional intelligence for the sake of discipline. Nope!

14

Don't *Go* through the Day, *Flow* through the Day
(Routines and Rituals)

Innate willpower is very rare. And our children, though full of capability and value, aren't likely to develop discipline without nurturing guidance. I mean, kids don't come into the world ready to brush their teeth and clean their rooms. So, the values you are teaching must be ingrained in the family culture consistently in order to help your child develop discipline. Otherwise, you're just expecting them to learn behaviors that aren't supported by their environment. This is where *routines and rituals* come in.

What Are Routines and Rituals?

While a routine asks "What will I do today?" a ritual asks, "What will I *feel* today?" Routines are for productivity tasks, while rituals are for tasks that evoke certain desirable states like joy, calm, and excitement. An 8:30 p.m. bedtime may be a part of your evening routine, but adding a ritual like prayer may help you and your children feel more grounded. The degree to which you prioritize one over the other will depend on your values, but I believe both are important.

When I first became an entrepreneur, I made my own schedule. My daughter was homeschooled and we went through our days with a lot of freedom. We definitely prioritized rituals much more in that season. Nowadays, however, I have a more intense workflow and my daughter is in school. And because we have chosen to make these changes, we are also choosing to adapt in ways that create more ease and flow. We have found security in creating more deliberate routines. The challenge has been to make sure we are still incorporating rituals so that we can still feel that sense of freedom within our new lifestyle. It's important to understand that no matter what your family system looks like right now, you can benefit from having both rituals and routines.

Creating Routines You'll Both Stick To

Before you transform your routines, it will be helpful to clarify what they actually are. Routines can be really supportive tools in your home. By establishing clear, consistent boundaries, you give your children something to expect within their environment. And a consistent environment encourages secure attachment and collaboration. So in order for your child to feel safe, there needs to be some level of consistency. When simple and flexible, routines can have powerful impacts on your relationship with your child. So how do you create routines that will actually work for you and your child?

1. **Figure out what the urgent repetitive tasks are in your day.** When your children are younger, you will have more influence over your routines. However, as they grow, it will be important to consistently be open to, and value, their input. So to whatever degree is appropriate, collaborate with your child to figure out what needs to be in your routines. In the morning, those things might be always brushing their teeth or eating breakfast. Urgent tasks in the afternoon might be completing homework and

cleaning their room. At night, it might be eating dinner and bath time. All of these present a certain level of urgency because, if ignored for too long, they will present tangible consequences.

2. **Once you've figured out all of the urgent repetitive tasks, consider the most conducive time blocks for each task.** It may require some experimentation to figure out how long each task takes and also the best time to do them in your day, but once you figure it out, you'll be able to create effective time blocks for each task. As you continue to be present with your family's specific needs, these time blocks will evolve, so stay flexible.

3. **Set up an environment that supports your routine.** The amount of tasks you and your child complete in a day doesn't really matter. It will be up to you to determine that. What's important is that you have enough support within your environment to help facilitate those tasks. If you have twenty tasks and a conducive environment, your routine is realistic. Conversely, if you have three tasks but your environment does not support them, the routine is not realistic. If you've established that it's "lights out" for your family sometime between 7:30 and 7:45 p.m., you will have to create boundaries within your environment to ensure that you and your children can do that consistently. If there is a ton of stimulation until 7:00 p.m., it may be difficult to get your children to wind down.

4. **Keep it flexible.** Rigidity and intimacy don't often mix well together. Seriously! Without flexibility, it's very hard to create strong connections with your children. You won't have time for the impromptu dance party if dinner has to be on the table at *exactly* 6:30 p.m. I recommend utilizing *time blocks* rather than specific times. For instance, if your child struggles with the bedtime routine and you have a rigid schedule, it will be difficult for you to stay connected, curious, collaborative, and communicative. However, if

you've built flexibility within the routine, you'll be much more likely to be able to show up with presence and openness. You may tell your child that bedtime is 8:00 p.m. while knowing that you've already allotted a twenty-minute window just in case you need it. Flexibility will also be important as the parent-child dynamic evolves. Your routines will be ever-changing as you move through different seasons in your lives. Your obligations will change. Your routine with a teenager won't look the same as your routine with a preschooler. You'll create moments of joy and connection in many different ways throughout your journey. So stay open to growth and transformation.

I've found engineering my environment for success to be extremely helpful for implementing a consistent routine with my daughter. We aren't naturally disciplined people. But I'm proud of how consistent we've become just by creating the best environment for us. When my daughter started school, we collaborated to figure out the best time for her to do her chores. Through some trial and error, we realized that she becomes less motivated to do her chores the later it gets in the day. We also recognized that her biggest distractions are electronics. (No surprise there!) So in order to make it easier for her to build a habit of getting her chores done, things like her computer and the television are simply inaccessible until she completes her chores. I remember that she's learning the values, so I don't leave things in her environment that aren't going to support her in developing discipline. Again, I can't expect a nine-year-old to have the willpower to do her chores consistently, so the phone and laptop are put out of sight until she's completed the dishes. It's built into the environment and routine so she knows what to expect every single day. I'm sure you can imagine what life looked like before we changed our environment. We struggled every single day! It seemed like I'd ask her a thousand times to wash the dishes, while she'd keep requesting just five more minutes on Super Mario. Either I'd end up unplugging the game or I'd just give in and the dishes wouldn't get done. Neither of us knew what to expect each day. We were doing it the hard way. Do yourself a favor and don't be like we were! Use boundaries to set up a supportive environment for the urgent tasks in your day. Think about ways you can make it easier for you all to follow the routine. Put the electronics away for a bit, keep the snacks up high until after dinner, put everything for the night routine in one easy-to-reach spot, and be willing to help them when they need it; do whatever makes sense for your family in order to create an environment that accommodates your routine.

Creating Rituals That Feel Good

Now let's talk about our rituals. A ritual is a type of routine that focuses on evoking certain feelings. There are deliberate actions that increase and maintain your family's well-being. What good is a completed to-do list if you and your child feel like crap, right? The to-do list itself isn't the reward, is it? I imagine you probably desire more from your day than a few checked-off boxes. I have found rituals to be the missing piece to the puzzle that creates more ease, flow, and peace throughout the day.

Now, we're typically pretty conscious of creating routines. There are pretty clear consequences when you neglect the *urgent* things for too long; it doesn't take long for a home to get completely out of order. It doesn't take long for the dishes and the laundry to pile up. You can *see* the results. Unlike urgent tasks, however, *important* tasks don't always have such obvious consequences. They insidiously affect our well-being, mental health, and emotional health, as well as our relationships with our families. So while routines ask "What do we want to do today?" rituals ask "How do we want to feel today?" Do we want to feel connected, confident, rejuvenated, calm, grateful, excited, grounded, joyful, collaborative, curious, relieved, playful, or something else? While you'll probably need to focus on things like chores and homework, you'll also want to schedule some important things like connecting with your child, teaching value-based lessons, playing and doing things that evoke joy and lightheartedness, experiencing quiet time and mindfulness, enjoying relaxation and rejuvenation, getting to know each other, learning new skills, increasing competence and confidence, and practicing emotional intelligence and effective communication. I'm sure you're doing most, if not all, of these things at some point, but are they prioritized the same way the urgent tasks are?

If you desire peace within your day, *schedule it.*

If you want to feel grateful, *make it a practice.*

If you are looking for more connection, *prioritize it.*

Rituals make the mundane tasks so much easier. If you were tapped into peace before you picked your child up from school, you'd probably respond to the afternoon tantrum much differently. If you were feeling grateful for the child you have, you'd probably respond to their homework struggles with more compassion and grace. Think about how much easier bedtime is (or might be) when your child feels calm and safe.

There's so much emphasis in our world on the external environment. We check off boxes all day long for small glimpses of joy and peace, but we tend to forget how much creative control we actually have over our days. No one will stop you from enjoying five minutes of meditation in the morning. There's no authority that will revoke your parenting card if you sing your child to sleep each night. *You* get to engineer your life in a way that is not only conducive to productivity but also conducive to the way you and your child want to feel.

So how do you take your routine and transform it with the power of rituals?

1. **Look at your typical tasks and ask how you both want to feel while you're doing them.** (It's a great idea to do this with your child.)

Focus on figuring out what you both need emotionally throughout your day by answering these questions:

- How do we want to feel when we wake up?

- How do we want to feel during the morning routine?

- How do we want to feel at school drop-off?

- How do we want to feel when completing family chores?

- How do we want to feel on the way to soccer practice?

- How do we want to feel during homework?

- How do we want to feel at bedtime?

- How do we want to feel during transitions with the co-parent?

- How do we want to feel during _____ ?

It can be pretty easy to deprioritize our mood states, but by doing so we basically hand over our well-being to whatever circumstances come our way. This goes back to our radical responsibility as intentional parents and managing the things we actually have some creative control over. Is everything in your control? Not necessarily. It would feel great if the girls and I could sleep in until 10:00 every morning. We would be so calm! But there would be some major consequences, because I'm not in control of what time school starts. There are many other things, though, that I can add to our morning routines to create more connection, joy, and peace. We get to decide what we eat, how we are woken up, what the first things are that we do in the mornings, and so many other things. When we choose these important things consistently, we can feel much more confident and delighted with our routines.

2. Once you've asked "How do we want to feel?" consider practical ways to evoke those feelings by asking questions like the following examples:

- How can I support myself to feel grounded before I wake the kids up?

- What are some things that will help both me and my children feel calm and connected before we start our day?

- Would it benefit me to do a reset meditation before I start the night routine?

- How can we feel more brave on the way to school?

- Is there a way to help my child feel safer every night?

- What can make chores feel super playful and stress-free?

- Should we make a playlist to get us pumped up on the way to practice?

- What can we try to relieve the anxiety around going back to Dad's house?

- How can we reconnect when you get home?

Maybe it's yoga, maybe it's snuggle time, or maybe you both go for an evening walk and talk about your day before homework time. Setting aside time within your routine to perform these rituals will make sure that the important things don't get overlooked. And honestly, it's a great way to make routines more enjoyable for both of you.

My older daughter and I used to really struggle with our nighttime routine. Sometimes, we would dreadfully move through each task and express an uninspiring "good night" at the end of the night. Other nights, we would play and connect throughout the routine and go to bed feeling grateful and connected. I really wanted to experience that intimacy more consistently, so I got intentional about infusing rituals into our nighttime routine. We wanted to feel calm, so we shut down external sensory stimuli in enough time for our brains and bodies to regulate before bed. We wanted to feel safe and connected, so I didn't just send her to bed; we would do some activity like reading a story, or a meditation, or having a quick chat about our day in her room right before she closed her eyes. Physical sensations help her to feel safe, so sometimes I would rub her back or snuggle up until she was cozy. Her willingness to move through bedtime is much greater ever since we started prioritizing these rituals.

3. **Set up your environment to support the added rituals.** Don't depend on willpower to make sure you prioritize your rituals. Find ways to have clear, tangible reminders of your rituals every day. If you and your child like to read before lights out, keep the books by the bed. If you like to send notes to school each day to help your child feel connected even while they're away, leave the pen and pad beside the lunch box so you have a visual cue each morning. Set sleep timers on your television and phones to remind you when it's time to start winding your brains down. Set alarms that remind you to tap into certain mood states throughout the day. (I have a 3:00 p.m. alarm that says "Joy Rampage." It's my daily reminder to shift into fun, lighthearted mode just before I pick up my girls. When that alarm goes off, I'll do a gratitude practice or listen to fun music to set the positive mood. Without that alarm, I'm likely to just check off the pick-the-girls-up box while in whatever mood I happen to be in.)

Discipline through routines and rituals doesn't just happen on its own. (Oh, how I wish we just had an internal system that ensured we took care of the urgent and important things, but it doesn't work that way, does it?) We have to tap in as intentional leaders in order to help our children cultivate discipline in our homes, and that's going to look different for all of us. Just remember to stay flexible, keep it simple, and create an environment that supports you.

15

Practice Makes Progress
(Rehearsing Behaviors)

Imagine a WNBA player waiting until game day to practice shooting a basketball. Or a gymnast waiting until the Olympics to learn how to do a back handspring. When you wait until chaotic moments hit to teach your children important skills, you're essentially doing the same thing—you're waiting until an inappropriate behavior occurs before trying to teach the appropriate alternative! But all of those wonderful skills you're trying to cultivate can actually be rehearsed on a regular basis. And when you and your child rehearse values-based behaviors in peaceful moments, they will be much easier to access when you both really need them. So, rather than waiting until game day or stressful moments to teach positive behaviors, consider what might happen if you *proactively prioritized practice*? (Say that five times fast!) Consider what would happen if, instead of waiting until a meltdown to teach calming breathing techniques, you used bedtime each night to practice this skill? What would happen if you didn't wait until you were completely overstimulated to ask for space? What if, instead, you practiced space breaks and independent play on a regular basis, even when you didn't really *need* a break?

Rehearsing Behaviors with Your Child

It can be difficult to learn a new skill, particularly if you haven't had consistent practice with it. But it can be much easier to get cooperation from our children in difficult moments when we are intentional about helping them rehearse positive behaviors in the easier moments. Of course, not every behavior requires rehearsal. (Thank goodness!) But you will know better than anyone the challenges that are consistently coming up in your home. Think about a challenging behavior your child is exhibiting. Are you proactively putting most of your effort into preventative measures to teach new behaviors or are you treating the symptoms after they arise? If you're waiting until your child breaks the fifth toy this month to teach them how to respect their things, they're going to have a really difficult time developing that skill.

One of my clients was really struggling with her ten-year-old's tantrums, so I recommended introducing rehearsal with her child to deal with her child's big feelings. I reminded her that calming techniques would be much more difficult for her daughter to access when she's already dealing with big emotions, but that she could support her in building the habit of emotional regulation through a daily practice that was implemented outside those triggered moments. She worked with her daughter to find a time where they could work on this skill proactively. She started using EFT (Emotional Freedom Techniques), meditation, and other mindfulness-based techniques with her daughter every night before bed. She also started having emotional intelligence conversations with her daughter every single afternoon after school. She would check in and ask how her daughter was feeling and give her an opportunity to effectively process her feelings and the events of her day. Does it mean that the tantrums completely went away? No. Her daughter's big feelings had deep roots, as she'd experienced some trauma. Her emotional state didn't happen overnight and it won't change overnight; however, her daughter slowly formed new habits and beliefs that supported the growth of her emotional intelligence. Before they began rehearsing these skills in calmer moments, it would be impossible for her to get her daughter to take deep breaths. Now she's able to sit with her daughter when she's upset and co-regulate with her. That's a major change and it happened because she was willing to rehearse calming tools with her daughter in moments when she didn't actually need them.

Rehearsing Behaviors with Yourself

You may have some positive behaviors that you are struggling to teach in high-stress moments because you are struggling to model them in those high-stress moments. For example, if you recognize that being present in the moment is a struggle for you, don't wait until you're burnt out after a long day to try to give your full attention to your kids. Instead, try building intentional moments of presence into your daily schedule. Try leaving your phone tucked away in your nightstand until your kids are out the door, on the bus, and headed to school so you can be fully present and attentive for all of those morning conversations and activities. Maybe you have "special time" right when they get home, where you sit and connect with them before you move into the nightly routine.

Personally, I can admit that apologizing to my kids is one of the hardest things for me to do. I don't take anything more seriously than I do my role as a parent. So when I mess up, I feel all the big feelings. And sometimes it takes me a while to step away from the shame story and say to myself, "Hey, everyone makes mistakes. Go in there and apologize to your kid." I recognize that this is something I have to work on, so I don't wait until I've hurt my daughter's feelings in a major way to practice saying I'm sorry. That's what I used to do and there were way too many moments when she got an apology long after the mistake because it was just so difficult for me to access accountability. Instead, I practice apologizing on a regular basis when I'm not caught in the shame story. When her feelings are hurt, even slightly, I practice saying, "I'm sorry," and I do so without providing excuses. I picked her up late for practice last week and I had a really good reason. I could have gone into why I picked her up late and she would have understood, but instead I just took accountability for not keeping my word. And fortunately for me, I'm not perfect, so there are endless opportunities in my day to apologize! I practice apologizing without excuses for the minor mistakes. I do this because in the moments when I mess up big-time and I'm really feeling like a shitty parent, she still deserves an apology. And I can't allow my shame or my excuses to be more important than her hearing me say and mean "I'm sorry." And so in order to make this a habit, I practice it often!

I remember a client who noticed she had a difficult time using kind language when she got upset. She told me that she wanted to find a way to still speak respectfully, even when she was triggered. So I asked her what "kind language" meant to her. She mentioned making gentle requests rather than forceful demands. So I asked her how she asked for things in a regular, untriggered moment. Did she ask or demand? That's when the light bulb came on for her. She realized that she used a demanding tone and every day would say things like "Give me the remote!" or "Go get your shoes!" She had developed the regular habit of making demands even in calm moments, so obviously she would follow that same pattern when she was triggered. She only just noticed the demands when she was triggered. She hadn't realized that she was regularly practicing the very same habit that she wanted to stop when she was triggered. Of course, it was a challenge for her to use kind language when she got frustrated, so we strategized on some ways that she could intentionally practice making gentle requests on a regular basis. She had to rehearse making gentle requests in moments when she wasn't triggered so she could slowly get better at it in the moments she (and her kids) needed it the most.

Building Rehearsal into Your Daily Routine

Remember, rehearsal allows us to teach our children values-based behaviors preventatively. That way, when crunch time happens, they're more prepared to rise to the occasion. You don't wait until you have company coming over to make a big deal about cleaning up. If cleanliness is one of your core values, it's something that you should rehearse consistently. If that's something you value, you need to create boundaries around cleaning on a daily basis. Don't wait until the room is a mess after three weeks of getting minimal attention to expect immediate cooperation. You have to find a way to work practice into your daily routine.

Here's how you can build rehearsal into your daily routine:

1. **Get curious about a few behaviors you'd like to start rehearsing.** Your child isn't a robot and you can't just program forty-five new behaviors onto their "hard drives." It's probably more realistic to instead focus on just a few developmentally appropriate behaviors at a time.

2. **Communicate with your kids.** Explain whatever you're trying to teach in a developmentally appropriate way. Collaborate on possible solutions and remind your children that they are your teammates. You can do anything together, including forming new habits. Put them at ease and let them know that you are committed to working together and supporting them through the process.

3. **Find the most connected times to practice.** There are moments in your day where your patience is much higher than others. It's in those moments that you'll want to rehearse new behaviors. For me, I'm most grounded when I pick my kids up from school, during individual time with them, and during bedtime. So I try to maximize those moments. Sure, we play and have fun, but I also use those moments to rehearse! When I pick my girls up from

school, my youngest takes a space break and rehearses independent play. While the youngest is doing independent play, I sometimes take that opportunity to practice calming techniques with the oldest. I'm a bit more regulated when it's just the two of us and, honestly, so is she. I could use that time to just chill and watch TV (which we often do), but I recognize how important cultivating emotional intelligence is, so I try my best to make intentional use of these moments. During bedtime I feel extremely calm and regulated, so that's when I take the opportunity to recap our day, practice being present, and actively listen to both of my girls. These things happen at some point in the day, almost every day.

4. **Maintain a growth mindset.** What we practice persists! You and your child *can* form new habits. Believe this! Even when you're struggling or have relapse moments, still believe that you're putting them in the best position possible through consistent rehearsal. When you prioritize practice, there will be growth. Sure, some behaviors will require a bit more time and effort than others, but the goal is progress, not perfection. Can you commit to patience? Are you willing to honor even the most subtle shifts in your or your child's behaviors? Are you willing to embody a growth mindset with your child? If you are, your child will feel that sense of hope and optimism and they will mirror it back to you. They can do hard things—with your support and consistent practice, of course!

16

You Messed Up! Now What?
(Making Repairs)

The final intentional parenting strategy is *repair*. I've saved it for last because it's the tool you'll lean on the most whenever you're struggling to be a connected, curious, collaborative, or communicative parent. As you begin to shift and become more of an intentional parent, you'll still make mistakes, and that's okay. In fact, I hope that's one of the strongest messages you take from this book—you *do not* have to be perfect! I wish I could whisper it in your ear every night before you go to bed and scream it at the top of my lungs when you get side eyes from judgmental family members! You get to mess up, because *everyone* does. I mess up every day. Whether I forget the theme day at school or tune my kid out while she's talking, I make mistakes all the time, so my children hear me say "I'm sorry" often.

You may have similar experiences where a simple apology and a hug do the trick. But what about those more challenging moments when you cause more significant harm? Depending on your child and the situation, an apology might not be sufficient. You know the kind of parent you want to be and you know there will be moments when your actions really miss that mark. It happens. I can't tell you of a single client or parent in my community who hasn't made what they feel was a big mistake in their parenting. And this is especially true for those of us who are dealing with our own traumas, going through difficult life transitions, or dealing with physical, mental, or emotional health challenges. And while I'm not saying you aren't responsible for your actions, I am reminding you once again that you don't have to be perfect. Your child doesn't need you to be perfect, either. They just need you to show up, keep learning, and take accountability when you inevitably mess up. You, like your child, still deserve grace. And your child deserves your empathy and compassion. Repair takes care of both. It's how we honor our humanness while still respecting theirs. It's about repairing whatever damage or harm may have been caused with our actions. Through repair, you get to show your children what healthy accountability looks like. You get to show them how to release shame about their mistakes so that they can grow as humans. You also get to show them how to have compassion for others.

Making Repair a Priority

Repair is probably one of the most important tools you can have as a parent. I like to use the following analogy to illustrate just how important it is. Think about putting on your favorite shirt. You love this shirt! It fits perfectly, you feel great in it, and you wear it more than any other shirt. Now visualize yourself about to take it off at the end of the day only to look down and notice that it has a hole at the bottom. It sucks, but it's a small hole, so it's still wearable. No one will notice! Plus, you love this shirt so much that you're not going to let a little hole stop you from wearing it again. You throw it in the washing machine, dry it, and fold it as usual. But you notice something the next time you go to wear the shirt. The hole got a little bigger. And over time, that little hole becomes a big hole. And before long your favorite shirt doesn't really feel the same. You don't feel as confident in it and it doesn't bring the same joyful feeling it used to. Whether you keep wearing it or decide to toss it out, you can't deny the shirt just isn't the same. This is what happens to our relationships when we neglect the repair process over and over again. It causes emotional holes and tears at the seams of our relationships. Even if the relationship is not completely damaged, it's not the same without repair.

Here's what makes repair difficult to practice, though. There's no one watching. No one is going to put you in a corner or issue you a fine because you didn't give your child a genuine apology. Even your child will eventually dust it off, come show you love, and continue on as if nothing ever happened. Children can be pretty forgiving in that way and they rarely demand repair from us. But does it mean they don't deserve it? Absolutely not. A shirt can be worn with a hole, but if that hole grows for too long, it will eventually become unwearable without some major repair. So when there's a hole in your relationship, don't ignore it—fix it! You don't want things to just *seem* better. Repair is the intentional practice of actually *making* things better. Repair is about healing and reclaiming whatever little pieces are lost in our triggered, unconscious parenting moments. But what exactly does repair look like in a practical sense? Well, I'm going to outline some steps for applying it to ourselves and our children, but first I want to tell you what repair *is* and what it *is not!*

- **Repair requires acknowledgment that harm was done.** Hearing you reflect back on what happened lets your child know that you understand the full extent of your mistake. Sometimes you won't know exactly what the harm is, so lean into curiosity to ensure that you can see your child's perspective and actually acknowledge the entirety of the mistake.

- **Repair is a commitment.** During the repair process, you can reestablish safety by outlining a clear plan of action for the future. If you yell at your child, you can tell them what actions you plan to take next time you're triggered. Or if you're not sure of what actions to take, you can tell them that you are committed to finding another tool for those moments in the future. (Of course, you need to make sure you actively seek out new tools.)

- **Repair happens only when you *both* are ready to do so.** It would be nice if you could jump into the repair process immediately after every mistake, but you won't always have the capacity to do so, particularly in the moments when emotions are high. You'll want your child to feel an incredible sense of safety within this process, so you have to make sure you are energetically up for the task. Of course, you shouldn't put it off forever, so if you're struggling to come back and take accountability for a mistake, take some intentional time to lean into a calming tool first so you can ground yourself and then begin the repair process with your child.

- **Repair is not just about issuing a quick "I'm sorry."** Children can sense an empty apology. You don't want to just brush over the repair process. Instead, you'll want to stop, get present, and show them how important it is to you.

- **Repair doesn't excuse behaviors.** You can't make excuses and take accountability for your actions all at the same time. When you make excuses, you are saying that your actions were out of your control. It's really hard to commit to future behaviors if we don't assert our responsibility over ourselves and our actions.

- **Repair doesn't come with expectations.** Your child may not forgive you right away. Can you still commit to the repair process even if it is not immediately received? Absolutely.

- **Repair does not happen without consent and connection.** If your child is not ready to engage in the repair process, listen to them and respect that. Recognize that you've done something to hurt them and accept that they may not feel safe, comfortable, or ready to receive your apology. (In these moments, I like to reestablish trust and connection before I start the repair process.)

Begin the Repair Process with Yourself First

As you parent with more intention, certain things you used to do unconsciously will no longer feel right. Behaviors like talking over your child, not considering their feelings, or calling them "bad" or "manipulative" won't feel the same. Yelling will feel different, too. You'll become more aware when you say things like "Stop crying" or "It's your fault I'm angry." You'll be more aware of when you're rushing through the day and not being present with your children. It doesn't mean you'll always have the consciousness to catch yourself, but through reflection, you will notice things you didn't previously. While this new level of awareness can be extremely helpful for forming new habits, it can also lead you toward more self-judgment, and that can make it really easy to go into the shame-and-blame stories in your head.

"This is my fault."

"I just keep messing up."

"I'll never be the parent I want to be."

Or my personal shame story that I used to carry with me...

"You have too much trauma to be a good mom." (Whatever the hell that even means.)

These stories can create some serious issues. First, they're just not helpful. You don't change from shame. Do you change through awareness? Yes! Through shame? No! Also, these stories don't take into account so many important factors that would prove them to be incorrect. Our shame stories are like the person who shows up after the fireworks and complains about the party being boring. That's what your shame stories are. They're faulty judgments! That doesn't make them less real, though, does it? There's an energetic, sometimes automatic reaction to our guilt that can transform it into shame. When this happens, you need to make a conscious effort to pause and mend things with yourself first. You don't want to bring shame into the repair process with your child. Imagine someone apologizing to you but focusing more on how *they* feel. "I'm so sorry. Oh my gosh, I'm literally the worst person ever. I keep doing this. I'm just hopeless." Yikes! And while it's totally understandable to feel that way, that kind of communication misses the accountability mark by a long shot. So before you can practice repair with your child, make sure you're not carrying any shame that is a result of the situation. If you are, please don't beat yourself up! I have so much compassion for you if you ever feel this way. Accountability is even harder when you feel ashamed, but know that the part of you that is intentionally showing up deserves repair, so make it a priority. You deserve to move forward in your parenting feeling safe, confident, and hopeful. Repair with yourself is really just the conscious act of self-forgiveness.

If you're struggling with shame related to a specific situation with your child, here's how you can repair it. Either in your head, speaking aloud, or writing in a journal, set aside time to move through the following process.

The Past

1. Review what happened in a very observational way. Don't make judgments.

   "When my daughter got in the car after school. She got in the car, slammed my door, and said 'Where's my phone?' I turned around, looked at her, and said, 'You didn't even

say "hello." I can't stand you sometimes.' I then rolled my eyes and drove off."

2. Consider what led up to your mistake. What was happening? What were you thinking? What were you feeling? (This information is for you to become more aware of what leads to reactive moments so you can be more present and proactive in the future. This is not information to use when apologizing.)

"I was so tired when I picked her up from school. I really have way less patience when I'm exhausted. I was needing rest and ease and I unintentionally put that responsibility on her. So when she got in the car and didn't acknowledge me in an "easy-going" way, I took it personally."

3. How did you feel immediately after you made the mistake?

"I felt even more tired after saying that to her. I also felt really overwhelmed and guilty. I'm angry with myself."

4. How do you think your child might have felt?

"I'm choking up just thinking about it, but I imagine she felt shame and sadness when I said that. She's probably also feeling angry, as well."

The Present

1. How are you currently feeling about what happened?

"I feel really ashamed of myself. I don't know why this keeps happening."

2. Do you feel this anywhere in your body?

"I feel this uneasiness in my stomach."

3. What do you need in order to feel safe, calm, and grounded right now?

"I'm going to take three belly breaths to ground myself. Then I'll get some water and maybe take a quick nap."

The Future

1. What could you do differently next time? (Commit yourself to a different response in the future.)

"I am going to find ways to rest proactively rather than waiting until I'm extremely exhausted and reactive."

2. Begin to forgive yourself by choosing a forgiveness statement that acknowledges all of the awareness you've gained through this process.

"I forgive myself for saying that I can't stand my beautiful, sweet, loving daughter. I know that this made me feel really guilty and it probably made my daughter feel a deep sadness. We both left the situation feeling very angry. To support myself, I'm taking long deep breaths. I forgive myself for saying this to her. I'm doing my best. I'm growing. And I am committing to self-care and rest so I can show up with more patience in the afternoons."

Does a forgiveness statement have to be long-winded like this one? Of course not, though I do recommend it, at least in the beginning. The more you practice this, the quicker you'll be able to forgive yourself. Eventually, you'll be able to quickly recognize what happened, acknowledge your feelings, decide what's going to be different in the future, and then give yourself a high-five and keep it moving! You may also get to a point where you no longer carry much shame and don't need to follow this process at all. I'm not there yet, but I'm working at it!

I hope this process brings you a lot of peace. Yes, I've outlined some clear steps you can follow, but this is just a general guide.

There's really no right or wrong way to forgive yourself. What matters most is alleviating the shame so you can show up to your child compassionately. If it happens to be through this process, great! If you can skip the internal dialogue and move right into using your calming tool with your child, that's great, too!

Repair with Your Child

Once you have acknowledged your mistake and given yourself compassion, you can extend that same compassion to your child. Remember: you must first get consent from them to do so. First, check in with them and see if they feel open enough to hear you or just try reading their body language. How are they responding to you? Are they communicating openness or something else? Sometimes after a challenging moment my daughter will barely look at me. She'll use a very monotone voice and give me short answers. This is not my daughter's normal behavior; it's a signal that our connection is off. This shows me she's not open. At other times, she may not show me with her body language. In these moments, I still find it important to ask "Are you open?" or "Can I talk to you about what happened earlier?" Whether she says "no" with her words or just with her body, I will back off the subject and try to connect with her first. Sometimes just sitting quietly together makes her feel safe. Sometimes just acknowledging and validating her feelings makes her feel safe: "I see you don't want to talk right now. I respect that so much and I'm open to talking whenever you are ready." Comments like that remind her that I value and respect her, and she can fall safely back into my arms whenever she feels comfortable doing so. Of course, you don't have to wait until your child is no longer upset, angry, scared, or sad to do repair. Consent just means they're open to listening and they're regulated enough to hear you. That's it.

So once you feel safe enough to speak and your child feels safe enough to listen, you can start the repair process. Keep in mind this isn't a linear process. Sometimes I start in the middle and sometimes I start at the end. As long as I acknowledge the "past, present, and future" in my repair, we both walk away feeling more connected and secure.

The Past

1. Explain what happened. (Just like with the self-repair process, make observations, not judgments.)

   "Earlier, I said I couldn't stand you."

2. Explain how they may have felt. (You can ask them how they felt or make empathetic guesses.)

   "How did you feel when I said that?"

   "I imagine you felt sad. Is that true?"

The Present

1. Express a very direct apology. Make it clear what you are taking accountability for.

   "I am so sorry that I said that. I do not think that was okay."

2. Figure out what they need now and how you can support them.

   "How can I support you right now?"

   "Is there anything you need right now?"

   "Can I help you with your big feelings?"

The Future

1. Get their input on future situations.

   "Is there anything you'd like me to do differently next time?"

2. Commit to a new behavior.

"In the future, I'm going to make sure I feel calm in my body so that I can be more compassionate toward you at pickup because that's what you deserve."

While repair is not a crutch to lean on so you can continually mess up, you should remember that you will never be a perfect parent. The only perfect parent is the one who lacks self-awareness, and that's not you. You know there will be moments of reactivity. You know you're going to make mistakes. But repair, when done thoughtfully, can have a greater impact than the mistakes themselves. (Go back and read that last sentence again.) Repair is the gift. It's an opportunity to expand our relationships with our children. It's how we teach them empathy, self-compassion, and accountability. It is the bridge we take that leads from mistakes to growth, and from disconnection to harmony.

A Letter to You, the Reader

I am so grateful to be a part of your journey. If you've made it this far, I hope you feel empowered to make positive changes in your life. However, I know that parenting advice can also bring up some shame. You may be wondering, "I don't know if I can really change. Can I really get control of my triggers? Can I really parent with more connection, curiosity, collaboration, and effective communication? Is it really possible to break the cycles I've unconsciously developed?" If any of this resonates, I want to offer you some insight.

You can still parent with intention from exactly where you are. The point of this book is to help you notice where you are, and do so without judgment. You have to be first willing to see your current experience with kind eyes so that you can transform it. Shame is the antagonist to your transformation and should be avoided at all costs. You *can* get control of your mental state. You do not have to be a victim of the lack of safety you've experienced in the past. You can learn to recognize the thoughts and emotions that are leading to your fight-or-flight behaviors before those thoughts and emotions take over. And the more you gently notice your thoughts and emotions steering you off course, the easier it will become to get back on track.

This is the beginning of what Dr. Daniel Siegel describes as *mindsight*. Mindsight is basically your ability to focus on your internal processes. It's looking at your thoughts, energy, and emotional experiences rather than just your external behaviors. If you grew up in an environment where people focused more on your behaviors, you may be disconnected from your internal experience.

Let me give you an example. If a child is bouncing on the couch and their caretaker just yells, "Get off the couch!" they miss an opportunity to look at what is happening in the child's brain and body. However, if the caretaker looks beneath the behavior they might respond like this: "It seems like you have a lot of energy right now. You can't jump on the couch. How about you go in the backyard and play for a bit!?" Rather than just fixing what is seen on the outside, the caretaker gives attention to what is happening in the child's body. So how does that translate in adulthood? If your experiences weren't reflected back to you in this way, you may be unconsciously controlled by your internal state rather than being able to control your internal state. So when a parent says, "I don't know why I can't stop yelling," this often signals to me a disconnect between their behaviors and the underlying causes in their bodies and brains. Struggling with mindfulness, problems with interpersonal relationships, and having a difficult time controlling your emotional state can result from years of being disconnected from your thoughts, energy, and emotional experiences. Luckily, you don't have to stay in this place. Dr. Siegel talks about *neuroplasticity*, which is a fancy way of saying that your brain is constantly making new connections. You are not bound to your past experiences or your current behaviors. You can grow your mindsight with practice. And by looking within and attending to your thoughts and emotions, you can create new neural pathways in the brain ultimately impact your behaviors. This is how we connect our internal experiences with our external world. This is how we create new narratives around our past experiences and present behaviors.

There are a lot of ways to do this. I'd like to share the four ways that I'm currently increasing my mindsight and ability to connect my underlying thoughts and emotions to my unhealthy behaviors. First, meditation allows me to get present and recognize my thoughts. I get to "watch my thoughts." This is incredibly helpful in reducing the anxious thoughts that I used to have throughout the day.

A Letter to You, the Reader

Checking in with my body when I'm triggered, as we discussed earlier in this book, is also a form of mindsight. Go back to the example with the child jumping on the couch. If a caretaker understands the underlying need for the child's body to release energy, they can offer healthy alternatives to the behavior. When I check in with my body before I respond to a trigger, I'm able to more consciously choose the behavior that follows. When I want to yell at my kids, I can go within and ask myself, "What are you feeling in your body and what are you thinking in your mind?" I can then connect my emotional experience with rational thought and proceed more consciously. I can witness my thoughts, acknowledge the angst in my body, find calm, and *then* respond.

With my highly trained EMDR (Eye Movement Desensitization and Reprocessing) therapist, I revisit painful memories in my childhood where my mindsight lens may have been fragmented. Through this therapy I've started to connect my mind and body to past experiences so that I can decrease the emotional charge. This has allowed me to start freeing myself from current patterns that resulted from my trauma.

Lastly, DBT (Dialectical Behavior Therapy) has been incredible in my journey. As I began focusing on my internal state, I became more conscious of my external behaviors. I was able to say, "Okay, Des! We're not going to do that." However, I soon realized I didn't know what I actually *should* do. I didn't have any healthy behaviors to replace the not so healthy ones. That's where DBT has been helpful. Through this skills-based approach, I've been able to strengthen my mindfulness, transform how I show up in interpersonal relationships, increase my ability to regulate my emotions, and build up my tolerance for distress and discomfort so that I don't respond from fight or flight.

Ultimately, you'll have to find what works for you. But I hope with all you've discovered in this book that you know that you are not a lost cause. You can stop yelling, build more discipline, become more emotionally available for your child, or accomplish whatever else it is that you're working on. Just remember: a house isn't built all at once. Every step, from the floors to the doors, is its own process and takes time. It's difficult. It's hard. But most importantly, you are capable.

Believing in you,

Destini

Index

Index

redirection and, 199
strengthening, 131–133
compassionate communication,
97, 187–188
calmness and, 98
clarity and, 98
courteousness and, 98
conflicting messages, teaching
and, 151–152
connection, 125–126.
See also relationships
compassion and, 129–130
flexibility, 128
growing together, 133–134
play and, 134–136
recapping and storytelling, 221
repairs and, 248
special time, 136–140
conscious awareness, 84–85
consent for conversation, 188,
248
consequences, collaboration and,
162
consoling, self-regulation and,
212
control
environmental safety, 67–79
survival mode parenting,
66–67
co-regulation, 206
calming tools, 217–218
S.O.U.N.D. (Slow, One,
Understand, Nudge, Do),
215–218
counseling, 87–88
critical thinking
communication opportunities,
190, 192
redirection and, 198
crying, trigger response, 109–110

curiosity, 143
recapping and storytelling, 222
what, 150–154
when
child's energy, 157–158
child's mood, 155–156
child's receptivity, 159–160
discipline, 154
rhythms, 154, 158
who, 144
consulting resources,
147–150
developmental stages,
145–147

D

DBT (dialectical behavior
therapy), 87
deep breathing, emotional
regulation, 121
de-schooling, 182
developmental stages
appropriate mistakes, trigger
response and, 117
collaboration and, 222
executive functioning and, 146
expectations and, 176–178
mission statement creation,
166
response to behavior and,
145–150
routine and, 243
rule following and, 110
dysregulation. *See*
regulating emotions

E

EFT (emotional focused therapy), 87

EFT tapping, emotional regulation, 121

EMDR (eye movement desensitization and reprocessing), 87

emotional intelligence, 209–210
  emotional regulation and, 206
  sympathizing and, 28–29

emotional regulation, 118
  autonomic nervous system, 119
  deep breathing, 121
  EFT tapping, 121
  emotional intelligence and, 206
  massage, 121
  neuroception, 119
  polyvagal theory, 120–121
  visualization and, 121

emotional safety, 80, 85
  The Bad Child storyline, 35–36
  journaling, 86–87
  mood tracking, 85–86
  play and, 135
  therapy, 87–88
  emotions. *See also* emotional regulation
  conscious awareness, 84–85
  rituals and, 233–238
  triggers and, 108–109

empathetic phrases for regulating emotions, 210

energy
  of child, curiosity and, 157–158

Joy Rampages, 63–64
  shifting, 61–64

environmental safety
  activities, 78–79
  boundaries and, 94
  finances, 68
  living arrangements, 69–72
  play and, 135
  relationships, 77–78
  routines and, 72–74, 231
  schedules and, 72–74
  support systems and, 74–77

executive functioning, 146–147

expectations, 176–178
  repairs and, 248

external shifts, 65

F

family as corporation,
  collaboration and, 163–164

family mission statement, 164–165
  display, 171
  planning, 166–169
  using, 171–172
  values
    listing core values, 169
    organizing into statement, 169–170
    questions to ask, 167–168

fawn response to triggers, 109, 119
  feeling seen, 59–61. *See also* presence

fight response to triggers, 109, 119
  co-regulation and, 206

fighting siblings, trigger response, 115

Index

awareness shifts, 54–55
boundary setting and, 92–104
collaboration, 179–180
communication and, 194
finances, 69
nonjudgment, 58
parenting intention setting
 and, 16–26
reflective journaling, 86
relationships, 77–78
shame, 250–252
stream-of-consciousness,
 86–87
support systems, 76–77
triggers, 108–118
Joy Rampages, 63–64
judgment
 The Black Sheep storyline,
 43–44
 self-regulation and, 213

K–L

kind language, 242

listening, active listening,
 184
living arrangements
 other occupants in home, 70
 space, 70
 tidiness, 69–70

M

massage, emotional regulation,
 121

MBCT (mindfulness-based
 cognitive therapy), 87
mistakes, developmentally
 appropriate, trigger response,
 117
mobilization (fight or flight),
 polyvagal theory, 120–121
mood of child, curiosity and,
 155–156
mood tracking, 85–86

N–O

needs
 boundary setting and, 92–93
 communicating, 95–96
 compassionate, 97–99
 confidence in, 99–100
 you-centered, 96
negative attention, shame and,
 35–36
neuroception, 119
"no" as response, 90
nonjudgment, shifting, 56–58
non-response, 183–184

observing without judging,
 209

P

parenting intention, 24–26
passions and interests, boundaries
 and, 94
perfectionism, The Good Child
 storyline, 29–31

Index

physical safety, regulating
  emotions and, 207
physical tools for calming, 218
play
  communication and, 193–194
  connection and, 134–136
polyvagal theory
  immobilization (dorsal vagal),
    120
  mobilization (fight or flight),
    120
  Polyvagal Ladder, 120
  social engagement
    (ventral vagal), 120
positive reinforcement, self-
  regulation and, 214–215
    power struggle diffuser. *See*
      redirection
practicing, prioritizing, 239
presence, 59–61
priorities
  rehearsals, 239
  repairs, 246–248
punishing, The Bad Child
  storyline, 34–38

Q

questioning, self-regulation and,
  214–215
questions, to encourage
  accountability, 226–227

R

recapping and storytelling, 220
  collaboration and, 222–223
  communication and, 222

connection and, 221
curiosity and, 222
fitness watch situation,
  223–227
receptivity of child, curiosity and,
  159–160
redirection, 197–199
  collaboration and, 199
  compassion and, 199
  critical thinking and, 198
  scenarios, 200–203
reflecting, communication and,
  184–187
reflective journaling, 86
  regulating emotions,
    118–122. *See also*
    co-regulation;
    self-regulation
  empathetic phrases, 210
  physical safety, 207
  recapping and storytelling,
    220–221
  S.A.F.E. (See, Accept, Find,
    Empathy), 208–210
  S.O.U.N.D. (Slow, One,
    Understand, Nudge, Do),
    215–218
rehearsing behaviors, 240–241
  implementing, 241–242
  kind language, 242
  as a routine, 243–244
    relationships, 77–78.
      See also connection
    boundaries and, 94
    intimacy and, 126
repairs, 245
  acknowledging harm, 247
  apologies, quick, 248
  child and, 253–254
  committing to, 247–248
  connection and, 248
  consent and, 248
  expectations, 248

Index

V

W

X–Y–Z

About the Author

Destini Ann Davis is a parenting coach and self-love radical who believes that in order to love, respect, and honor our children, we must first learn to love, respect, and honor ourselves. Her mission is to remind parents of all backgrounds of their innate power to parent from a place of compassion and understanding so they can then pass those same gifts along to their children. Through her popular TikTok, YouTube, and Instagram channels, she challenges parenting norms by offering safe spaces where parents can have frank conversations about difficult topics. She teaches with empathy and empowers parents to shift the cultures of their homes to parent with more grace, presence, and intention. She's a compassionate and relatable resource for parents from all backgrounds and she takes the psychology of parenting and turns it into fun, digestible content for her community.

From the public school system to her own home, Destini Ann has been developing her connection-based parenting approach for over 10 years. She has seen firsthand how the dynamics of a family can be transformed through intentional, empowered parenting. And she doesn't shy away from the difficult topics like single parenting and "mom guilt." Instead, she sheds light on the messiness of parenting and reminds parents of their personal power, regardless of their circumstances. In a society where parents are more stressed than ever, Destini Ann's heartfelt approach reminds us of the power of presence, empathy, and playfulness.